SCHOLASTIC

TIMES TABLES

TEACHER'S BOOK

AGES 9–11

Scholastic Education, an imprint of Scholastic Ltd

Book End, Range Road, Witney, Oxfordshire, OX29 0YD

Registered office: Westfield Road, Southam, Warwickshire CV47 0RA

www.scholastic.co.uk

© 2018, Scholastic Ltd

123456789   8901234567

British Library Cataloguing-in-Publication Data

A catalogue record for this book is available from the British Library.

ISBN 978-1407-18274-2

Printed and bound by Bell & Bain

All rights reserved. This book is sold subject to the condition that it shall not, by way of trade or otherwise, be lent, hired out or otherwise circulated without the publisher's prior consent in any form of binding or cover other than that in which it is published and without a similar condition, including this condition, being imposed upon the subsequent purchaser.

No part of this publication may be reproduced, stored in a retrieval system, or transmitted, in any form or by any means, electronic, mechanical, photocopying, recording or otherwise, other than for the purposes described in the content of this product, without the prior permission of the publisher. This product remains in copyright.

Due to the nature of the web we cannot guarantee the content or links of any site mentioned.

We strongly recommend that teachers check websites before using them in the classroom.

Every effort has been made to trace copyright holders for the works reproduced in this book, and the publishers apologise for any inadvertent omissions.

Author
Paul Hollin

Editorial
Rachel Morgan, Shannon Keenlyside, Audrey Stokes, Helen Lewis and Julia Roberts

Cover and Series Design
Scholastic Design Team: Nicolle Thomas, Neil Salt and Alice Duggan

Layout
Claire Green

Illustrations
Matt Ward @ Beehive Illustration

CONTENTS

	Introduction	4
1	**Mastering the times tables**	10
2	**Practising the times tables**	21
3	**Investigating the times tables**	43
4	**Extending and applying the times tables**	50
	Additional resources	60

Scholastic Times Tables

The National Curriculum in England expects all children to be taught to recall the multiplication and division facts for multiplication tables up to 12 × 12. From June 2020, all children in England will also take an online timed multiplication tables check, up to and including 12 × 12, at the end of Year 4. This means that, more than ever, a firm grasp of the times tables is key.

It is also important to keep in mind that, for many children, the time spent trying to master the times tables may define how they view themselves as mathematicians. A focus on rapid recall can increase anxiety, not only with multiplication, but with other areas of maths. Conversely, rapid recall of times tables can be confused with deep understanding of multiplication and division; children may move on to new concepts too quickly, causing problems in understanding later on.

These factors make it all the more important that we get right how we teach, and how children learn, the times tables. *Scholastic Times Tables* provides a wealth of rich and varied activities in the *Teacher's Book* and engaging recaps and practice in the *Practice Book*. These work alongside our diagnostic and timed digital practice to help you and your children not only reach National Curriculum expectations but develop a deep understanding of multiplication. The following strategies should be used to get the best results.

Building understanding

- **Provide opportunities for exploration and reasoning** Scholastic Times Tables *Teacher's Book* offers a rich variety of activities to get your children thinking about the times tables in a meaningful way. Children should explore ideas, building on what they already know to develop a deeper understanding of multiplication. The *Practice Book* offers varied practice as well as providing further opportunities to develop their problem-solving and reasoning skills (see page 7).

- **Represent multiplication visually** When exploring any multiplication table, it is important that children are continually exposed to the different ways in which multiplication can be represented, such as number lines, arrays, counters, number frames, number rods and base-10 equipment. Use these throughout Key Stage 1 **and** 2 as part of your whole-class teaching. Encourage children of **all abilities** to use them to model and check their work as well as explore ideas and patterns.

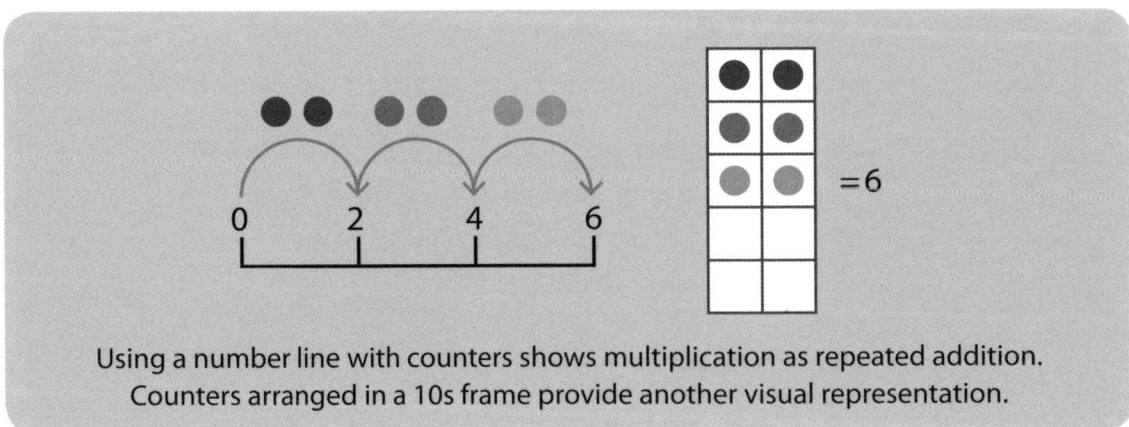

Using a number line with counters shows multiplication as repeated addition. Counters arranged in a 10s frame provide another visual representation.

- **Promote talk and discussion** Many of the activities in this book, as well as the *Practice Book*, ask children to explore an idea and explain their thinking. Shift the focus away from talking only when you think you know the 'right' answer by explaining that talking is a great way to work through a problem as it helps us to work out what we do and do not know. Sharing your ideas with someone else is even better!

- **Find patterns and draw connections** Move away from talking about 'tricks' and making things 'easy' (for example *Multiplying by 10? Easy! Put a 0 on it!*) and instead focus on finding patterns and using what you already know to build understanding. Allow children to discover and test these patterns themselves, finding out what works and what doesn't. For example *$2 \times 4, 4 \times 4, 8 \times 4$. What do you notice? Could you use this to predict the answer of 16×4?*
- **Use what they know to learn more** Build on the connections in the tables. Continue to emphasise these links even after all the tables have been introduced.

Developing rapid recall

- **Practise in short bursts, often** Rather than devoting a longer chunk of time to rehearsing the times tables, aim to fit short sessions of practice into your day. Even a minute is enough time to fit in a quick all-class chant of a times table.
- **Make it fun** Use engaging and low-stress activities to encourage children to commit their times tables to memory, building their confidence and fluency. For example challenge children to set the times tables to music or make up a times tables rap!
- **Keep it bubbling** Children will use the times tables across many areas of maths and in everyday life. Continue to revisit even when you think they have learned them by heart.
- **Consider carefully when to test** Timed practice can be stressful for many children. Reiterate that understanding is most important and that speed will come with time and practice. Provide opportunities for low-stakes timed practice; this will help them to get used to being tested without the fear of failure. Challenge children to compete against their own personal best time rather than against that of others.

The components
Teacher's Book

The *Scholastic Times Tables Teacher's Book* provides you with a wealth of activities to help your children master the times tables. Work through the activities one by one or dip in and out – whatever works best for you and your class!

Choose from a bank of activities which promote problem-solving, reasoning and fluency. Aim to use a range of activities so that children have an opportunity to approach the times tables in a variety of ways.

The activities use a wide range of resources: some rely on using concrete resources, others have a whiteboard component to them, and others may require a photocopiable resource which can be downloaded from www.scholastic.co.uk/timestables-resources. Finally, some require no resources at all.

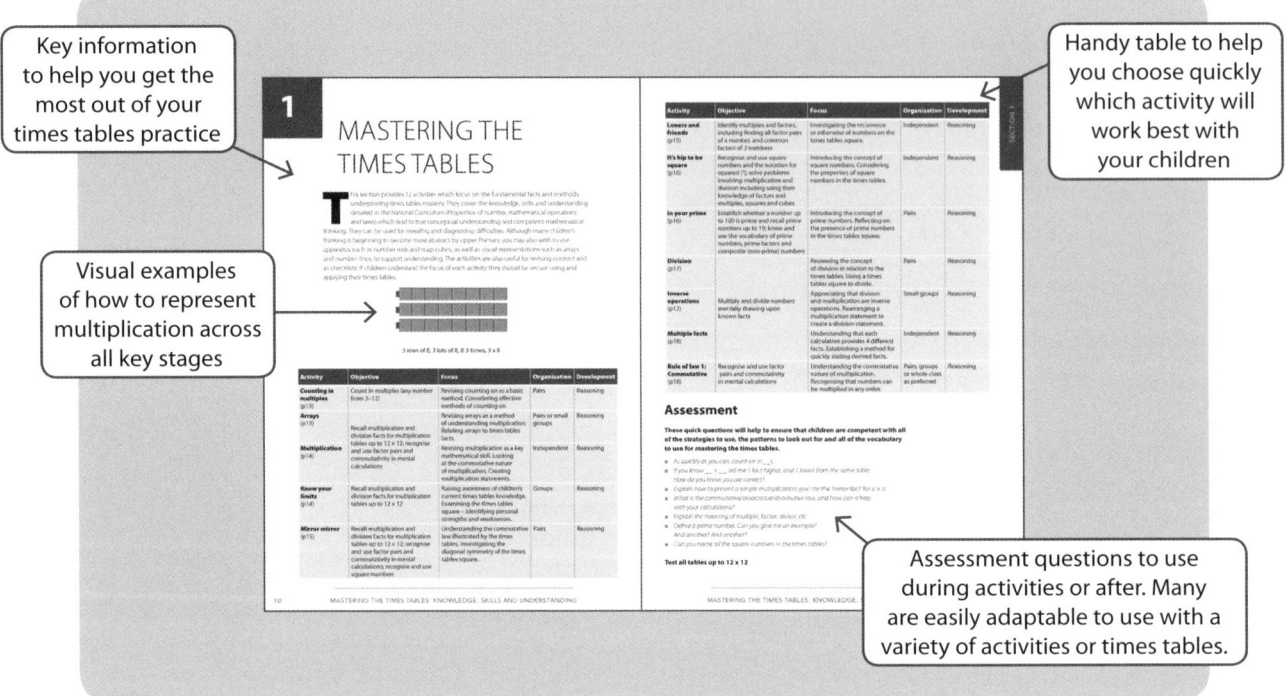

Key information to help you get the most out of your times tables practice

Visual examples of how to represent multiplication across all key stages

Handy table to help you choose quickly which activity will work best with your children

Assessment questions to use during activities or after. Many are easily adaptable to use with a variety of activities or times tables.

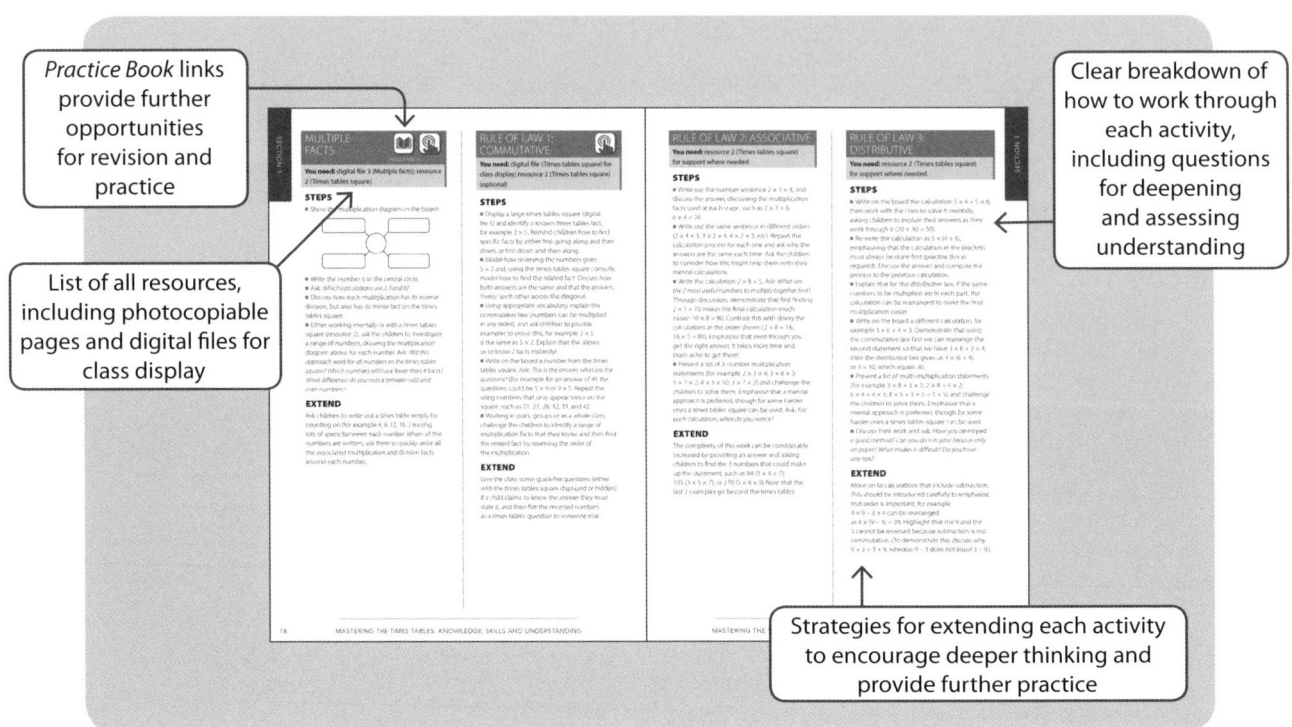

Practice Book links provide further opportunities for revision and practice

List of all resources, including photocopiable pages and digital files for class display

Clear breakdown of how to work through each activity, including questions for deepening and assessing understanding

Strategies for extending each activity to encourage deeper thinking and provide further practice

The *Practice Book*

The *Scholastic Times Tables Practice Book* has been designed to provide children with further opportunities for revision and practice of the times tables.

Use it alongside the *Teacher's Book*, as part of general class practice or for home learning. Look for the *Practice Book* icon 📖 in the 'You will need' section at the start of an activity for activities which relate directly to the *Times Tables Practice Book*.

Detailed answers are included at the back of the book.

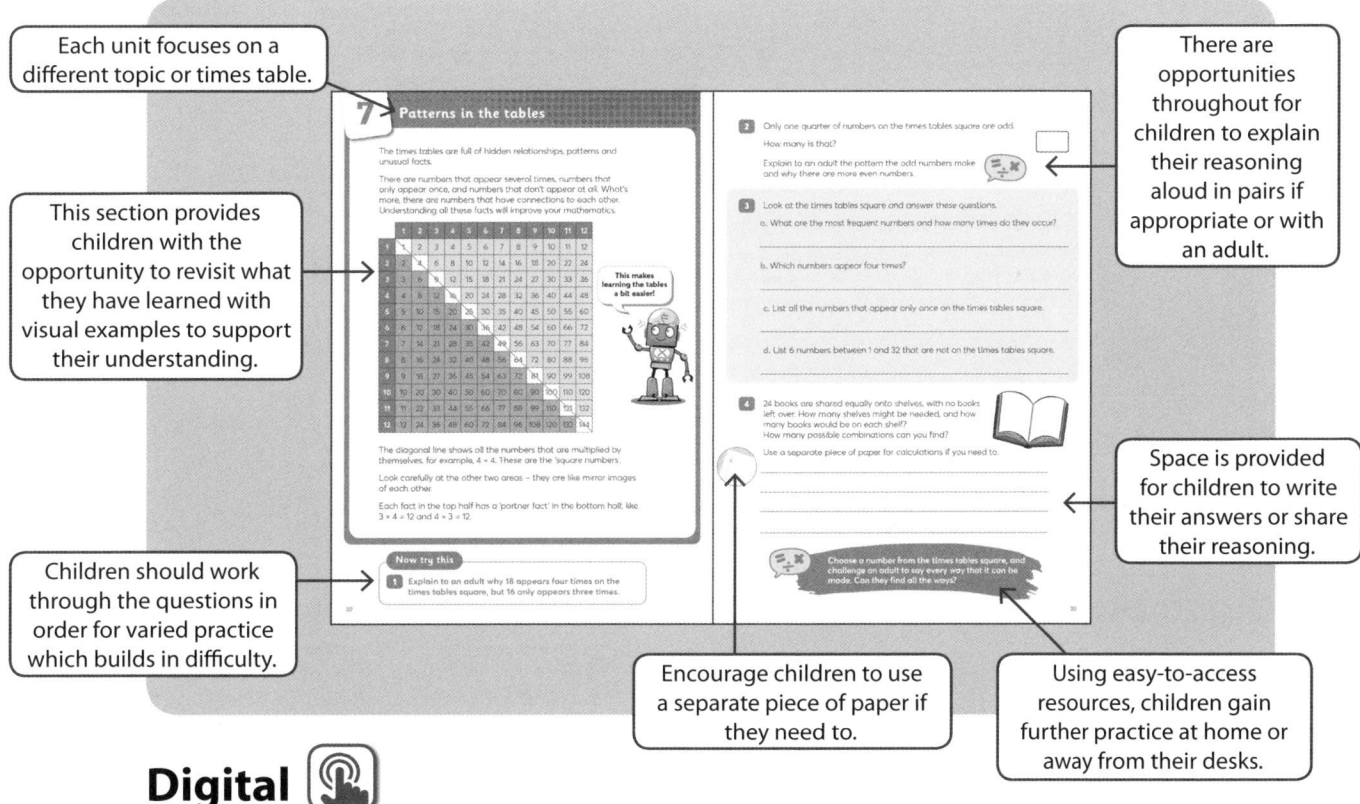

- Each unit focuses on a different topic or times table.
- This section provides children with the opportunity to revisit what they have learned with visual examples to support their understanding.
- Children should work through the questions in order for varied practice which builds in difficulty.
- There are opportunities throughout for children to explain their reasoning aloud in pairs if appropriate or with an adult.
- Space is provided for children to write their answers or share their reasoning.
- Encourage children to use a separate piece of paper if they need to.
- Using easy-to-access resources, children gain further practice at home or away from their desks.

Digital

Additional materials for this book can be found online at the following address: **www.scholastic.co.uk/timestables-resources** these include:

- resource pages including games and worksheets
- supporting PowerPoint digital files for display during your classroom teaching
- quick-fire written tests for additional practice or homework. These tests have three levels of differentiation and are aligned with a unit or group of units from the *Teacher's Book*. Assign one of the three sections at a time and progress through them in order.

If resource pages or digital files are required, they will be listed in the 'You will need' section at the start of an activity. Look for the digital icon 👆 for activities using digital content.

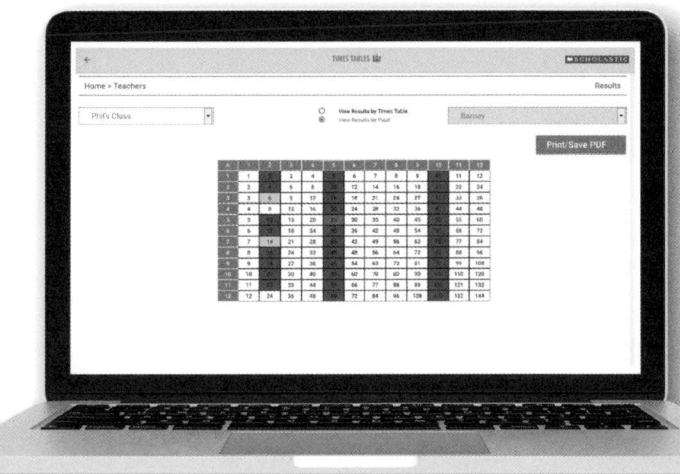

The digital *Times Tables Check* is included on a USB stick as part of the Classroom Pack, it follows the format of the National Times Tables Check. It can be used to inform your teaching and to provide practice in the test format. Frequently dipping in and out of the program will allow you to gauge progress as well as improving children's familiarity and reducing any associated anxiety that may arise from such checks.

The *Times Tables Check* is customisable, allowing you to select which times tables you would like to include in the check (1–12), the number of questions given and how long children have to complete it. Set up your class then adjust the class settings or individual settings to tailor the check to your children's needs. Use the reporting features to track children's progress and pinpoint areas for additional support. In addition, there is a practice area for children to explore which is not tracked in the reporting area.

The teacher settings are password protected with the password: **login**. A full how to use guide can be found on the USB stick or in the teacher's area of the program.

To install the content, insert the USB stick into a USB port on your computer.
For Windows users, if the install program does not start automatically, navigate to the USB drive, double click the installer program icon and follow the instructions.

For Mac users, navigate to the USB drive and double click the disk image file on the USB drive to mount it. In the window that opens, drag the application file icon to the applications folder icon.

Recommended system requirements:
USB type A port
Windows 7 and later are supported
MacOS 10.9 and above are supported (64bit only)
An internet connection is required for some program features.

Curriculum map

Scholastic Times Tables has been designed to meet the aims of the National Curriculum for mathematics in England to ensure that all pupils:

- become **fluent** in the fundamentals of mathematics, including through varied and frequent practice with increasingly complex problems over time, so that pupils develop conceptual understanding and the ability to recall and apply knowledge rapidly and accurately
- **reason mathematically** by following a line of enquiry, conjecturing relationships and generalisations, and developing an argument, justification or proof using mathematical language
- can solve **problems** by applying their mathematics to a variety of routine and non-routine problems with increasing sophistication, including breaking down problems into a series of simpler steps and persevering in seeking solutions

Mathematics is an interconnected subject in which pupils need to be able to move fluently between representations of mathematical ideas. The programmes of study are, by necessity, organised into apparently distinct domains, but pupils should make rich connections across mathematical ideas to develop fluency, mathematical reasoning and competence in solving increasingly sophisticated problems. They should also apply their mathematical knowledge to science and other subjects.

The expectation is that the majority of pupils will move through the programmes of study at broadly the same pace. However, decisions about when to progress should always be based on the security of pupils' understanding and their readiness to progress to the next stage. Pupils who grasp concepts rapidly should be challenged through being offered rich and sophisticated problems before any acceleration through new content. Those who are not sufficiently fluent with earlier material should consolidate their understanding, including through additional practice, before moving on.

The activities in this book cover the Programme of Study (statutory requirements) in Number: Multiplication and division for the following year groups:

Year 5

Pupils should be taught to:

- identify multiples and factors, including finding all factor pairs of a number, and common factors of 2 numbers
- know and use the vocabulary of prime numbers, prime factors and composite (non-prime) numbers
- establish whether a number up to 100 is prime and recall prime numbers up to 19
- multiply numbers up to 4 digits by a 1- or 2-digit number using a formal written method, including long multiplication for 2-digit numbers
- multiply and divide numbers mentally, drawing upon known facts
- divide numbers up to 4 digits by a 1-digit number using the formal written method of short division and interpret remainders appropriately for the context
- multiply and divide whole numbers and those involving decimals by 10, 100 and 1000
- recognise and use square numbers and cube numbers, and the notation for squared (^{2}) and cubed (^{3})
- solve problems involving multiplication and division, including using their knowledge of factors and multiples, squares and cubes
- solve problems involving addition, subtraction, multiplication and division and a combination of these, including understanding the meaning of the equals sign
- solve problems involving multiplication and division, including scaling by simple fractions and problems involving simple rates

Year 6

Pupils should be taught to:

- multiply multi-digit numbers up to 4 digits by a 2-digit whole number using the formal written method of long multiplication
- divide numbers up to 4 digits by a 2-digit whole number using the formal written method of long division, and interpret remainders as whole number remainders, fractions, or by rounding, as appropriate for the context
- divide numbers up to 4 digits by a 2-digit number using the formal written method of short division where appropriate, interpreting remainders according to the context
- perform mental calculations, including with mixed operations and large numbers
- identify common factors, common multiples and prime numbers
- use their knowledge of the order of operations to carry out calculations involving the 4 operations
- solve addition and subtraction multi-step problems in contexts, deciding which operations and methods to use and why
- solve problems involving addition, subtraction, multiplication and division
- use estimation to check answers to calculations and determine, in the context of a problem, an appropriate degree of accuracy

1 MASTERING THE TIMES TABLES

This section provides 12 activities which focus on the fundamental facts and methods underpinning times tables mastery. They cover the knowledge, skills and understanding detailed in the National Curriculum (Properties of number, mathematical operations and laws) which lead to true conceptual understanding and competent mathematical thinking. They can be used for revealing and diagnosing difficulties. Although many children's thinking is beginning to become more abstract by upper Primary, you may also wish to use apparatus such as number rods and snap cubes, as well as visual representations such as arrays and number lines, to support understanding. The activities are also useful for revising content and as checklists: if children understand the focus of each activity they should be secure using and applying their times tables.

3 rows of 8, 3 lots of 8, 8 3 times, 3 x 8

Activity	Objective	Focus	Organisation	Development
Counting in multiples (p13)	Count in multiples (any number from 2–12)	Revising counting on as a basic method. Considering effective methods of counting on.	Pairs	Reasoning
Arrays (p13)	Recall multiplication and division facts for multiplication tables up to 12 × 12; recognise and use factor pairs and commutativity in mental calculations	Revising arrays as a method of understanding multiplication. Relating arrays to times tables facts.	Pairs or small groups	Reasoning
Multiplication (p14)		Revising multiplication as a key mathematical skill. Looking at the commutative nature of multiplication. Creating multiplication statements.	Independent	Reasoning
Know your limits (p14)	Recall multiplication and division facts for multiplication tables up to 12 × 12	Raising awareness of children's current times tables knowledge. Examining the times tables square – identifying personal strengths and weaknesses.	Groups	Reasoning
Mirror mirror (p15)	Recall multiplication and division facts for multiplication tables up to 12 × 12; recognise and use factor pairs and commutativity in mental calculations; recognise and use square numbers	Understanding the commutative law illustrated by the times tables. Investigating the diagonal symmetry of the times tables square.	Pairs	Reasoning

Activity	Objective	Focus	Organisation	Development
Loners and friends (p15)	Identify multiples and factors, including finding all factor pairs of a number, and common factors of 2 numbers	Investigating the recurrence or otherwise of numbers on the times tables square.	Independent	Reasoning
It's hip to be square (p16)	Recognise and use square numbers and the notation for squared (^{2}); solve problems involving multiplication and division including using their knowledge of factors and multiples, squares and cubes	Introducing the concept of square numbers. Considering the properties of square numbers in the times tables.	Independent	Reasoning
In your prime (p16)	Establish whether a number up to 100 is prime and recall prime numbers up to 19; know and use the vocabulary of prime numbers, prime factors and composite (non-prime) numbers	Introducing the concept of prime numbers. Reflecting on the presence of prime numbers in the times tables square.	Pairs	Reasoning
Division (p17)		Reviewing the concept of division in relation to the times tables. Using a times tables square to divide.	Pairs	Reasoning
Inverse operations (p17)	Multiply and divide numbers mentally drawing upon known facts	Appreciating that division and multiplication are inverse operations. Rearranging a multiplication statement to create a division statement.	Small groups	Reasoning
Multiple facts (p18)		Understanding that each calculation provides 4 different facts. Establishing a method for quickly stating derived facts.	Independent	Reasoning
Rule of law 1: Commutative (p18)	Recognise and use factor pairs and commutativity in mental calculations	Understanding the commutative nature of multiplication. Recognising that numbers can be multiplied in any order.	Pairs, groups or whole class as preferred	Reasoning
Rule of law 2: Associative (p19)	Recognise and use factor pairs and commutativity in mental calculations; for example use the distributive law $39 \times 7 = 30 \times 7 + 9 \times 7$ and associative law $(2 \times 3) \times 4 = 2 \times (3 \times 4)$	Understanding the associative laws. Organising numbers in multiplication statements to make mental calculations easier.	Independent	Reasoning
Rule of law 3: Distributive (p19)		Understanding the distributive law. Organising calculations with more than 1 multiplication.	Independent	Reasoning
Talk proper (p20)	Pupils should read, spell and pronounce mathematical vocabulary correctly	Developing children's use of correct mathematical vocabulary. Using mathematical terms when explaining concepts.	Small groups	Reasoning
How many numbers? (p20)	To develop awareness of the table as a whole	Investigating different numbers in the times tables.	Pairs or small groups	Reasoning

MASTERING THE TIMES TABLES: KNOWLEDGE, SKILLS AND UNDERSTANDING

Assessment

These quick questions will help to ensure that children are competent with all of the strategies to use, the patterns to look out for and all of the vocabulary to use for mastering the times tables.

- *As quickly as you can, count on in __s.*
- *If you know __ × __, tell me 1 fact higher, and 1 lower from the same table. How do you know you are correct?*
- *Explain how to present a simple multiplication; give me the 'mirror fact' for a × b.*
- *What is the commutative/associative/distributive law, and how can it help with your calculations?*
- *Explain the meaning of multiple, factor, divisor, etc*
- *Define a prime number. Can you give me an example? And another? And another?*
- *Can you name all the square numbers in the times tables?*

Test all tables up to 12 x 12

COUNTING IN MULTIPLES

You need: digital file (100 square) for class display, or a large number line; resource 9 (100 square); counters; snap cubes

STEPS

- Display a large 0–30 number line or a 100 square (digital file) and demonstrate counting on as a way of solving some 2-times table questions (for example 3 2s: 2, 4 ,6)

- Explain the concept of counting in multiples as repeated addition: adding on the same amount each time.
- Use a range of quick-fire questions for the 2-, 3-, 4- and 5-times tables, and count with the class up to a maximum of 10 times depending on class competence at this stage.
- In pairs, children practise solving times tables questions by counting on. They can use a 100 square (resource 9) and counters to 'mark' each counting on (for example 5 8s: 8, 16, 24, 32, 40).
- Ask: *As you count along, what other times tables facts do you encounter? What would be the next fact you encounter? Can you count up to 12 multiples of any number?*
- Try covering the multiples of a chosen number with counters, all the way up to 12 times, then with these numbers hidden try counting on.
- All of the above can be adapted to counting backwards in multiples as a way of introducing repeated subtraction and division.

EXTEND

Using sets of snap cubes, such as 3 lots of 5, demonstrate the link between counting on and repeated addition. In pairs, children can compare the efficiency of each method, that is, does it vary between easier and more difficult times tables? Ask: *Is counting on always, sometimes, or never more efficient than repeated addition?*
This can also be adapted to cover repeated subtraction as counting back, as in the main activity.

ARRAYS

You need: counters or cubes

STEPS

- Draw a set of dots on the board (for example 2 rows of 4 dots) and ask the class what the array represents (2 × 4 and 4 × 2 are both acceptable). Elicit that the total is 8.
- Repeat this for a range of smaller times tables facts, and discuss with the class what is useful about this method – it helps you visualise the calculation; and what is trickier – it is not so useful for larger numbers. Can the children explain why?
- Give pairs or groups of children a collection of counters. Ask them to state an answer (for example 10) and then challenge each other to create 1 or more arrays that matches it (for example *If the answer is 10, what could the array be?* 5 × 2, 2 × 5, 10 × 1, 1 × 10)
- Ask: *For an array, what happens if you add another row or column? Can you use this for a whole times table? What about using arrays for division – are they useful?*

EXTEND

Draw on the board a large array of 12 × 12 dots. Challenge the class to investigate how they might find 2 different arrays that make up the whole 12 × 12 grid, and then another, and another. Then ask them to write down the calculations that their arrays present. Do these arrays relate to each other in any way? (They should always total 144.)

MULTIPLICATION

You need: snap cubes

STEPS

- Using snap cubes, demonstrate the concept of 'lots of', such as 3 lots of 2 makes 6.

- Use the same cubes to illustrate different statements (1 lot of 6; 2 lots of 3; 6 lots of 1). Try using colours to help with this (1 lot of 6 – all red; 2 lots of 3 – 3 blue, 3 yellow; 6 lots of 1 – 6 different colours).
- Ask the children to explain the mathematical statements they have written, such as $2 \times 3 = 6$; $6 \times 1 = 6$. Ask them to consider why these are equivalent to each other, and reflect on how the same number can be made in different ways.
- Give children a quantity of cubes and challenge them to create, for example 6 different multiplication statements by creating 'lots of' cubes, and to then write each set as a multiplication.
- Ask: *What happens if you remove 1 of your lots? What about removing 2 lots? What other facts can you use your 'lots' to help you with (1 fact fewer, 1 fact more)?*

EXTEND

Ask the children to use a fixed number of cubes to create a multiplication fact and its commutative fact (for example 4×3 and 3×4). Can they spot any strategies for doing this quickly? (This is about realising that the arrangements of cubes form arrays. If they ignore the colouring of cubes they can simply rotate their connected set of cubes through 90º to make the commutative fact.

KNOW YOUR LIMITS

You need: digital file 1 (Know your limits) for class display; resource 2 (Times tables square) (optional)

STEPS

- This activity should be done regularly (for example half-termly) to help children monitor their own learning.
- Display a large times tables square (digital file 1) and discuss its characteristics, reviewing correct uses through modelling and quick-fire questions (What is 4 3s? How do we make 25? What are 7 lots of 6?)
- Spend time discussing anything children notice about the square, such as its diagonal symmetry.
- Explain that secure times tables facts are those that can be explained instantly. Then, working with children in groups, ask the children to assess their own knowledge. Ask them to each think of 1 hard and 1 easy fact. They then share and explain why they think they find them hard and easy. Do the others in their group agree? Can they suggest ways to remember other people's hard facts? Which tables facts do they know instantly, which require further work?
- Challenge the children to teach each other their method for learning facts they are secure with.
- Ask: *Which of your tables are secure? Why do you think they are secure? Which do you need to work on? Why do you think that? Can you give me a secure fact and then explain an insecure fact? Use a secure fact to help you to deduce another fact. And another and anothe?*

EXTEND

Ask children to pinpoint specific tables facts they cannot recall, either across the whole times tables square, or for a specific table. Challenge them to learn 1 or more facts for the next day, and to share a strategy for trying to recall it.

MIRROR MIRROR

You need: digital file (Times tables square) for class display, or a large number line; resource 9 (100 square); resource 2 (Times tables square)

STEPS

■ Display a large times tables square (digital file 1) and, through class discussion, elicit that there is a diagonal line of symmetry within it, from top left to bottom right.

	1	2	3	4	5	6	7	8	9	10	11	12
1	1	2	3	4	5	6	7	8	9	10	11	12
2	2	4	6	8	10	12	14	16	18	20	22	24
3	3	6	9	12	15	18	21	24	27	30	33	36
4	4	8	12	16	20	24	28	32	36	40	44	48
5	5	10	15	20	25	30	35	40	45	50	55	60
6	6	12	18	24	30	36	42	48	54	60	66	72
7	7	14	21	28	35	42	49	56	63	70	77	84
8	8	16	24	32	40	48	56	64	72	80	88	96
9	9	18	27	36	45	54	63	72	81	90	99	108
10	10	20	30	40	50	60	70	80	90	100	110	120
11	11	22	33	44	55	66	77	88	99	110	121	132
12	12	24	36	48	60	72	84	96	108	120	132	144

■ Spend time discussing how this works as a line of symmetry and what this means for numbers above and below it on the square, highlighting appropriate numbers, such as 20 (4 × 5 and 5 × 4). Work through various examples, using prompts such as: 6 × 5 = 30. Ask: *What other times tables fact does this give us? Can you use this fact to find another fact near to it, 1 higher or lower? And another, and another?*

■ Using individual times tables squares (resource 2), ask pairs to investigate how they can rapidly find the 'mirror' of any fact. Then, without the times tables square as a prompt, ask children to fire statements at each other such as 3 × 5 = 15, and then use their 'mirror knowledge' to state the related fact.

EXTEND

Challenge the children to focus only on the central diagonal line – from 1 × 1 to 12 × 12. Ask them to discuss what they notice about the numbers on this line. Are any of the numbers elsewhere on the square? Is there anything unusual about the numbers? (This is looking for knowledge of square numbers.)

LONERS AND FRIENDS

You need: digital file (Times tables square) for class display; a copy of resource 1 (Times table facts) for each child

STEPS

■ Display a large times tables square (digital file 1), highlighting the diagonal line of symmetry from top left to bottom right. In discussion, elicit that although there are 144 numbers on the times tables square, some of them occur more than once. Can children explain why this might be?

■ Ask: *If 6 is the answer, what is the question? Repeat this for 4, 5 and 25.*

■ Ask: *How many times does the number 6 appear on the square? (4 times)* Discuss why this is the case (1 × 6, 6 × 1, 2 × 3, 3 × 2). Repeat this for 4 (3 times), 5 (twice) and 25 (once).

■ Give children copies of times tables facts (resource 1), ideally 1 per person, though paired work is also possible. If preferred, this can be displayed and done as a whole-class activity.

■ Ask the class to work through the questions on the worksheet – all or some – and then discuss findings, encouraging the children to explain their answers and to try and reason through their mistakes.

■ Ask: *Why should 25 occur only once* (its only factor is 5), *yet 24 occurs 6 times* (factors 2, 3, 4, 6, 12)*? Why is 15 on the square* (factors 3, 5)*, but not 17* (prime number)*? Which is the odd 1 out: 12, 13, 14 or 15?* (13 is not on the table)

EXTEND

Find the most frequently occurring numbers on the times tables square (12 and 24, 6 times each) and investigate the different ways they are made. Encourage children to explain why this is the case.

IT'S HIP TO BE SQUARE

You need: digital file (Times tables square) for class display; digital file 2 (It's hip to be square); paper; scissors

STEPS

- Write the square numbers 1, 4, 9, 16 and 25 on the board, Ask: *What do you notice about these numbers? Can you count in multiples to make them? What times tables facts do you know that include these numbers?*
- Display a large times tables square (digital file 1). Ask: *Can you see the numbers on this square? What about numbers larger than 5? Gradually elicit all the square numbers up to 144.*
- Explain that these are like the backbone of the times tables square. They act as the mirror line and all the other facts have symmetrical partners either side of them. Use explanations and questions as desired to illustrate this (for example 3 × 5 is 'opposite' 5 × 3).
- Initiate an investigation of the square numbers, using digital file 2 (It's hip to be square). Demonstrate with each click of the presentation how the square becomes larger and look at the corresponding times tables fact that supports each square.
- Ask the children to repeat this process using squares cut from cm² paper. Ask them to keep going until they have all 12 squares, counting or calculating the number of small squares in each area.

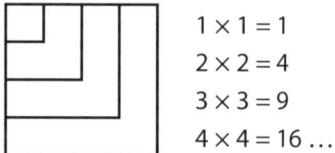

1 × 1 = 1
2 × 2 = 4
3 × 3 = 9
4 × 4 = 16 …

- Ask: *Can you find a relationship between the square numbers?* Work to elicit that the pattern is odd/even/odd/even…, and that the square numbers increase in a regular way – **1** + 3 = 4; **4** + 5 = 9; **9** + 7 = 16; and so on.
- Ask: *Can you describe this pattern? Why is this the case? What might it tell us about the tables?* (They are a grid of hidden patterns and links, defined by the basic properties of numbers, and mathematical laws.)

EXTEND

Write the squares of the numbers 1–10 and challenge the children to investigate any hidden relationships (the difference between the squares gets larger by 2 each time; also, $3^2 + 4^2 = 5^2$, and $6^2 + 8^2 = 10^2$).

IN YOUR PRIME

You need: digital file (Times tables square) for class display; resource 2 (Times tables square)

STEPS

- Write the prime numbers 2, 3, 5, 7 and 11 on the board. Ask: *What do you notice about these numbers? Can you count in multiples of a number to make 1 of them?*
- Explain the concept of a prime number – divisible only by itself and 1 (noting that 1 is not a prime number and that 2 is the only even prime number).
- As a class, discuss each of the numbers 1 to 12 and note the primes (2, 3, 5, 7 and 11).
- Display a large times tables square (digital file 1) or use 1 individual times tables square per child (resource 2). Ask children to find these first few prime numbers on it. What do the children notice about their occurrences and location on the times tables square?
- Tell the class that "a prime number greater than 12 will not be on the square". In pairs, ask the children to decide if this statement is true or not (and if they think there is a prime number greater than 12, where is it on the square, and if not, why not). Children should create a convincing argument to verify this. (There are no primes greater than 12 as prime numbers are not multiples of any number other than themselves.)
- Ask: *Define a Prime number. Is 1 a prime number? What is special about 2? What prime numbers can you spot on the times tables square?*

EXTEND

Challenge the children to identify any prime numbers between 12 and 30 (13, 17, 19, 23, 29). Discuss how they identified them, and how they can be sure they are primes.

DIVISION

You need: digital file (Times tables square) for class display; resource 2 (Times tables square); counters or cubes

STEPS

- Using counters, demonstrate fundamental division, for example take 6 counters and say 6 shared between 2 is 3. Model the familiar division format in writing (6 ÷ 2 = 3). Repeat as necessary.
- Display a large times tables square (digital file 1) and demonstrate how to use this to find such divisions. So, for 6 ÷ 2 we go to 2 on the vertical column on the left, move across until we find 6, and then move up to find the answer (3). Repeat as necessary, asking children to challenge a partner to find given facts.
- Working in pairs with a times tables square (resource 2), challenge children to find 10 division facts in a set time limit. Ask them to write each one down in the division format as modelled above. Ask: *Can you find a strategy for converting multiplication facts to division facts?* (and vice versa)
- As a class, share work and ask: *For any division fact, can you find another fact from the same multiplication table?* (For example if you have found 6 ÷ 2 = 3, you can quickly find 8 ÷ 2 = 4).
- Give a number, for example 4, and ask: *This is the answer, what is the (division) question?*
- Play 'True or False', working only with division. For example ask: *True or False, 48 ÷ 6 = 7.*

EXTEND

Choose a number from 1 to 12 and ask children to write down the complete 'division table' (all 12 facts). Either using their table or hiding it, ask quick-fire questions: *Give me a division fact from the 4-times table, and another, and another.*

INVERSE OPERATIONS

You need: snap cubes

STEPS

- Arrange some snap cubes to make a simple array, writing the multiplication statement for it, for example 4 × 2 = 8. Repeat as necessary for different arrays.
- Take 1 of the completed arrays (such as 3 × 5) and write the relevant multiplication statement. Keeping the array in sight, ask the children to consider how the same array can be used to create a division statement (for example 3 × 5 = 15; 15 ÷ 3 = 5). Again, repeat as necessary.
- Working in small groups with, if possible, 24 snap cubes in each group, challenge children to make visual representations of as many multiplication statements as possible *and* a connected division statement for each one.
- Note that children may make the connection to the 4 facts that arise from such numbers (for example 2 × 3 = 6, 3 × 2 = 6, 6 ÷ 3 = 2, 6 ÷ 2 = 3).
- To conclude, quick-fire a range of multiplication facts at the class and ask them to write down the accompanying division statement for each one. Ask: *Can you spot the relationship between multiplication and division? Can you convert a division fact to give you a multiplication fact?*

EXTEND

Choose a times table and ask children to write it in a column as fast as they can. Then, in a column next to it, ask them to write the equivalent 'division table', again as fast as they can.

MULTIPLE FACTS

PAGES 8 AND 9

You need: digital file 3 (Multiple facts); resource 2 (Times tables square)

STEPS

- Show the multiplication diagram on the board:

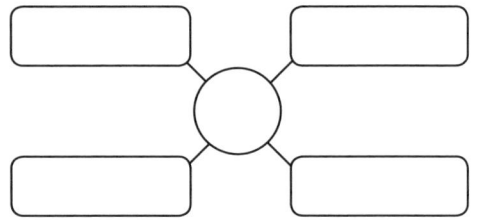

- Write the number 6 in the central circle.
- Ask: *Which calculations use 2, 3 and 6?*
- Discuss how each multiplication has its inverse division, but also has its 'mirror fact' on the times tables square.
- Either working mentally or with a times tables square (resource 2), ask the children to investigate a range of numbers, drawing the multiplication diagram above for each number. Ask: *Will this approach work for all numbers on the times tables square? Which numbers will have fewer than 4 facts? What difference do you notice between odd and even numbers?*

EXTEND

Ask children to write out a times table simply by counting on (for example 4, 8, 12, 16...) leaving lots of space between each number. When all the numbers are written, ask them to quickly write all the associated multiplication and division facts around each number.

RULE OF LAW 1: COMMUTATIVE

You need: digital file (Times tables square) for class display; resource 2 (Times tables square) (optional)

STEPS

- Display a large times tables square (digital file 1) and identify a known times tables fact, for example 2 × 5. Remind children how to find specific facts by either first going along and then down, or first down and then along.
- Model how reversing the numbers gives 5 × 2 and, using the times tables square correctly, model how to find the related fact. Discuss how both answers are the same and that the answers 'mirror' each other across the diagonal.
- Using appropriate vocabulary, explain the commutative law (numbers can be multiplied in any order), and ask children to provide examples to prove this, for example 2 × 5 is the same as 5 × 2. Explain that this allows us to know 2 facts instantly!
- Write on the board a number from the times tables square. Ask: *This is the answer, what are the questions?* (for example for an answer of 45 the questions could be 5 × 9 or 9 × 5. Repeat this using numbers that only appear twice on the square, such as 21, 27, 28, 32, 33, and 42.
- Working in pairs, groups or as a whole class, challenge the children to identify a range of multiplication facts that they know, and then find the related fact by reversing the order of the multiplication.

EXTEND

Give the class some quick-fire questions (either with the times tables square displayed or hidden). If a child claims to know the answer they must state it, and then fire the reversed numbers as a times tables question to someone else.

RULE OF LAW 2: ASSOCIATIVE

You need: resource 2 (Times tables square) for support where needed

STEPS

- Write out the number sentence 2 × 3 × 4, and discuss the answer, discussing the multiplication facts used at each stage, such as 2 × 3 = 6; 6 × 4 = 24.
- Write out the same sentence in different orders (2 × 4 × 3, 3 × 2 × 4, 4 × 2 × 3, etc). Repeat the calculation process for each one and ask why the answers are the same each time. Ask the children to consider how this might help them with their mental calculations.
- Write the calculation 2 × 8 × 5. Ask: *What are the 2 most useful numbers to multiply together first?* Through discussion, demonstrate that first finding 2 × 5 = 10 makes the final calculation much easier: 10 × 8 = 80. Contrast this with doing the calculations in the order shown (2 × 8 = 16, 16 × 5 = 80). Emphasise that even though you get the right answer, it takes more time and brain-ache to get there!
- Present a list of 3-number multiplication statements (for example 2 × 3 × 4; 3 × 8 × 3; 5 × 7 × 2; 4 × 3 × 10; 3 × 7 × 2) and challenge the children to solve them. Emphasise that a mental approach is preferred, though for some harder ones a times tables square can be used. Ask: *For each calculation, what do you notice?*

EXTEND

The complexity of this work can be considerably increased by providing an answer and asking children to find the 3 numbers that could make up the statement, such as 84 (3 × 4 × 7); 105 (3 × 5 × 7); or 270 (5 × 6 × 9) Note that the last 2 examples go beyond the times tables.

RULE OF LAW 3: DISTRIBUTIVE

You need: resource 2 (Times tables square) for support where needed

STEPS

- Write on the board the calculation 5 × 4 + 5 × 6, then work with the class to solve it mentally, asking children to explain their answers as they work through it (20 + 30 = 50).
- Re-write the calculation as 5 × (4 + 6), emphasising that the calculation in the brackets must always be done first (practise this as required). Discuss the answer and compare the process to the previous calculation.
- Explain that for the distributive law, if the same numbers to be multiplied are in each part, the calculation can be rearranged to make the final multiplication easier.
- Write on the board a different calculation, for example 3 × 6 + 4 × 3. Demonstrate that using the commutative law first we can rearrange the second statement so that we have 3 × 6 + 3 × 4, then the distributive law gives us 3 × (6 + 4), or 3 × 10, which equals 30.
- Present a list of multi-multiplication statements (for example 3 × 8 + 3 × 3; 2 × 8 + 4 × 2; 6 × 4 + 4 × 3; 8 × 5 + 3 × 5 + 1 × 5) and challenge the children to solve them. Emphasise that a mental approach is preferred, though for some harder ones a times tables square can be used.
- Discuss their work and ask: *Have you developed a good method? Can you do it in your head or only on paper? What makes it difficult? Do you have any tips?*

EXTEND

Move on to calculations that include subtraction. This should be introduced carefully to emphasise that order is important, for example 4 × 9 − 3 × 4 can be rearranged as 4 × (9 − 3) = 24. Highlight that the 9 and the 3 cannot be reversed because subtraction is not commutative. (To demonstrate this discuss why 9 + 3 = 3 + 9, whereas 9 − 3 does not equal 3 − 9.)

MASTERING THE TIMES TABLES: KNOWLEDGE, SKILLS AND UNDERSTANDING

TALK PROPER

You need: digital 4 (mathematical vocabulary)

STEPS

- Note: You may find it beneficial to return to this activity regularly, in short bursts, to both break down content and to aid consolidation of knowledge.
- Display digital file 4 (Talk proper). Talk through 2 or 3 of the items, discussing the meaning and the examples given. Expand on each definition with multiple examples as desired.
- Selecting 1, 2 or 3 of the terms, (or more if preferred) ask the children to work in small groups to create a brief presentation that explains each of their given term to someone who doesn't know about it. For example they might present the facts as if to an alien, or take the role of a mathematics professor using the language to maximum academic effect.
- Emphasise that it is essential that their presentation should include multiple examples (and not the ones shown on the worksheet). Children should present these on a flip-chart or as a PowerPoint slideshow. Groups should consider roles carefully and ensure that their efforts are coordinated and meaningful.

EXTEND

Write a selection of mathematical statements on the board for whole-class viewing. Use the examples from Talk proper (digital file 4) as a starting point but do not display the terms next to the example statements. For each statement, before solving it ask: *What can we say about this statement? What mathematical terms can we use to describe it? What laws should we use to solve it?* Use the opportunity to model the correct language and processes.

HOW MANY NUMBERS?

PAGE 22

You need: digital file (Times tables square) for class display; resource 2 (Times tables square)

STEPS

- This is a straightforward activity to help clarify the limited scope of the times tables square.
- Display a large times tables square (digital file 1) and discuss its general properties: there are 144 squares on it (more if you count the focus number along the top and down the side); each number has a 'twin' apart from the diagonal of 'square numbers'; some numbers occur more than twice, and some numbers only appear once.
- Working in pairs or small groups, challenge the children to use times tables squares (resource 2) to investigate, in total, how many different numbers there are on the square altogether. Ask: *Can you explain a strategy you can use for eliminating repeated numbers?* (For example using the commutative law, $3 \times 5 = 15$, so $5 \times 3 = 15$.)

EXTEND

Challenge children to categorise the different numbers in any ways they can. Ask: *How many odd numbers are there? How many even numbers? Which numbers are not in the times tables square? Explain your findings.*

Test all tables up to 12 x 12

PRACTISING THE TIMES TABLES

2

This section provides 3 activities for each times table: 1 each for *fluency*, *reasoning* and *problem-solving.* They are useful for children who need further support, but also for children already competent with their tables. Ongoing practice and thinking around them will help consolidate their skills. As such, activities can be used with individuals or groups for children who need help in some way or with the whole class as lesson warm-ups and introductions, refresher or revision sessions. Continue to use concrete resources such as number rods and visual supports to support children with conceptual understanding.

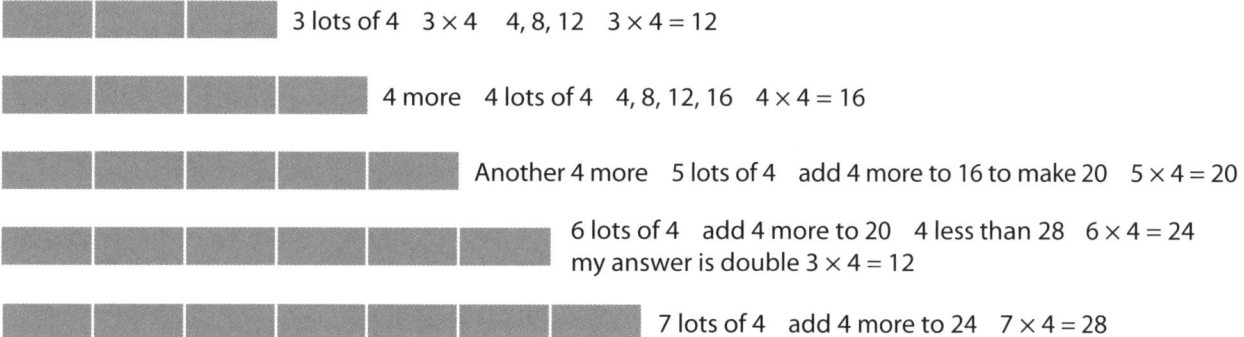

Activity	Objective	Focus	Organisation	Development
2-times table: Step 2 it! (p25)	Count in multiples (2s)	Revising the 2-times table by rapidly counting on and back in 2s. Oral fluency in counting in 2s.	Independent; small groups for extension	Fluency
2-times table: Pairs tower (p25)	Recall multiplication and division facts for multiplication tables up to 12 × 12	Developing sequential and non-sequential awareness of 2-times table facts. Visualising in 2s.	Pairs	Reasoning
2-times table: 2's company (p26)	Solve problems involving multiplying and adding	Using the 2-times table to solve problems. Combining different tables facts.	Pairs	Problem-solving
3-times table: Triplets (p26)	Count in multiples (3s)	Revising the 3-times table. Counting on and back in 3s. Oral fluency.	Small groups	Fluency
3-times table: 3's company (p27)	Recall multiplication and division facts for multiplication tables up to 12 × 12	Strengthen understanding of 3-times table facts. Using 3-times table facts to group numbers.	Small groups	Reasoning
3-times table: Stools-r-us (p27)	Solve problems involving multiplication and division	Solving problems for the 3-times table. Using the 3-times table for multiplication and division.	Independent	Problem-solving

PRACTISING THE TIMES TABLES: TABLE BY TABLE, FLUENCY, REASONING AND PROBLEM-SOLVING

Activity	Objective	Focus	Organisation	Development
4-times table: Pattern spotting (p28)	Multiply and divide numbers mentally drawing upon known facts	Using a repeating pattern to support mastery.	Small groups	Fluency
4-times table: Fingers and thumbs (p28)	Recall multiplication and division facts for multiplication tables up to 12 × 12	Identifying 4-times table facts from given numbers. Representing numbers with multiples of 4.	Groups of 6	Reasoning
4-times table: Odd ones out (p29)	Solve problems involving multiplication and division	Finding related 4-times facts. Investigating relationships between facts.	Pairs	Problem-solving
5-times table: Gimme 5 (p29)	Count in multiples (5s)	Revising the 5-times table by counting on in 5s. Counting to 60 in 5s, then identifying specific times tables facts.	Groups of 13 in a large space	Fluency
5-times table: Tally ho! (p30)	Recall multiplication and division facts for multiplication tables up to 12 × 12	Relating counting in 5s to times tables facts. Using tally charts as a starting point for the 5-times table.	Whole class	Reasoning
5-times table: Hand in glove (p30)	Solve problems involving multiplication and division	Using the 5-times table to solve problems. Recall and manipulation of 5-times table facts.	Individual, paired or groups as desired	Problem-solving
6-times table: Pack of 6 (p31)	Recall multiplication and division facts for multiplication tables up to 12 × 12	Rapid recalling of 6-times table facts. Consolidation of uncertain facts.	Pairs	Fluency
6-times table: Tumbling dice (p31)		Applying 6-times table facts. Making decisions to select 6-times table facts.	Small groups	Reasoning
6-times table: Hen power (p32)	Solve problems involving multiplication and division	Solving simple problems using 6-times table facts. Deriving times tables facts from given numbers.	Independent, paired or groups as desired	Problem-solving
7-times table: Knowledge building (p32)	Recall multiplication and division facts for multiplication tables up to 12 × 12	Improving recall of individual table facts. Revising strategies for learning and recalling the 7-times table.	Independent	Fluency
7-times table: Getting to know you (p33)		Honing strategies for reciting 7-times table facts. Using other times tables to help learn harder 7-times table facts.	Pairs	Reasoning
7-times table: Dear diary (p33)	Solve problems involving multiplication and division	Solving simple problems using the 7-times table. Dividing within the 7-times table.	Small groups	Problem-solving
8-times table: Have I seen you b4? (p34)	Recall multiplication and division facts for multiplication tables up to 12 × 12	Understanding the pattern of the 8-times table. Using a repeating pattern to support mastery.	Pairs	Fluency
8-times table: Happy clappy (p34)	Count in multiples (8s); recall multiplication and division facts for multiplication tables up to 12 × 12	Silently counting in 8s. Identifying sounds as cues for times tables visualisation.	Whole class	Reasoning
8-times table: Spiderama (p35)	Solve problems involving multiplication and division	Using the 8-times table to solve problems. Using division facts to derive answers.	Independent	Problem-solving

Activity	Objective	Focus	Organisation	Development
9-times table: Get handy (p35)	Count in multiples (9s); recall multiplication and division facts for multiplication tables up to 12 × 12	Rapidly counting in multiples of 9. Embedding the pattern of the 9-times table.	Independent, extension pairs	Fluency
9-times table: Pointers and patterns (p36)	Recall multiplication and division facts for multiplication tables up to 12 × 12; multiply and divide numbers mentally drawing upon known facts	Learning and using strategies for remembering 9-times table facts. Spotting and using patterns.	Pairs or small groups	Reasoning
9-times table: Packing boxes (p36)	Solve problems involving multiplication and division	Using 9-times table facts to solve problems. Identifying the nearest fact less than a given total.	Small groups	Problem-solving
10-times table: 10 out of 10 (p37)	Count in multiples (10s); recall multiplication and division facts for multiplication tables up to 12 × 12	Recalling and using multiplication facts for the 10-times table. Counting forwards and backwards in 10s.	Independent and pairs	Fluency
10-times table: Spot the genius (p37)	Recall multiplication and division facts for multiplication tables up to 12 × 12	Rapidly identifying multiplication facts for the 10-times table. Understanding the underlying mathematics when multiplying any number by 10.	Individual	Reasoning
10-times table: Stocking up (p38)	Solve problems involving multiplication and division	Applying the 10-times table facts. Using the 10-times table in a practical context.	Independent	Problem-solving
11-times table: Rapido! (p38)	Recall multiplication and division facts for multiplication tables up to 12 × 12; counting in multiples (11s)	Fluent recalling and reciting of the 11-times table. Rapid counting on and back in multiples of 11.	Whole class	Fluency
11-times table: Say what you mean (p39)	Pupils should read, spell and pronounce mathematical vocabulary correctly	Using correct vocabulary in discussing multiplication facts. Explaining the 11-times table.	Pairs	Reasoning
11-times table: Football crazy (p39)	Solve problems involving multiplication and division	Solving problems using 11-times table facts. Extended problem-solving activity.	Independent, paired or groups as desired	Problem-solving
12-times table: Different strokes (p40)	Recall multiplication and division facts for multiplication tables up to 12 × 12	Improving recall of individual 12-times table facts. Distinguishing between easy- and hard-to-remember facts on the 12-times table.	Whole class	Fluency
12-times table: Explain yourself (p40)		Developing awareness of 12-times table facts. Thinking about facts individually and assigning reasons for knowing any 1 fact.	Small groups	Reasoning
12-times table: Baking buns (p41)	Solve problems involving multiplication and division	Using 12-times table facts to solve problems beyond the 12-times table. Recall and manipulation of table facts.	Pairs or small groups	Problem-solving
Bingo! (p41)	Recall multiplication and division facts for multiplication tables up to 12 × 12	Rapid, correct use of a times tables square. Rapid use of times tables square for any multiplication facts.	Independent	Fluency

Activity	Objective	Focus	Organisation	Development
Table detectives (p42)	Recall multiplication and division facts for multiplication tables up to 12 × 12; solve problems involving multiplication and division including using their knowledge of factors and multiples, squares and cubes	Deducing times tables facts from indirect clues. Stating facts other than the obvious.	Whole class or paired work as preferred	Reasoning
This and that (p42)	Solve problems involving multiplication and division	Solving problems using all times tables facts. Applying and combining facts to calculate totals.	Independent	Problem-solving

Assessment

This section has covered all of the times tables, from 2 to 12. Assessment of children's fluency will ideally have been going on throughout. As well as using sample tests from the digital component and the *Practice Book*, the depth of children's understanding (as opposed to instant recall of facts) should be supported with appropriate open-ended questioning. For example:

- *Here is a multiplication fact: (for example 3 × 7 = 21). Give me 3 related facts.*
- *Tell me 4 ways of making 20 with the times tables.*
- *How do the 5 and 10 times tables* (or 3 and 6, 4 and 8, etc) *relate to each other?*
- *Which are the hardest tables to learn? Why?*
- *Why do some numbers appear several times* (or once, or not at all) *in the tables?*
- *What strategies do you have for learning harder facts?*
- *As quickly as you can, count on in __s.*
- *If you know __ × __, tell me 1 fact higher, and 1 fact lower from the same table.*
- *If __ × __ = ___, give me 3 other facts, 1 ×, 2 ÷*
- *Think of a times tables fact. Can you double/halve it?*
  What other facts can this 1 help you with? Does this fact link to other tables?

2-TIMES TABLE: STEP 2 IT!

You need: digital file 5 (Step 2 it)

STEPS

- Review the 2-times table and look at the pattern in it; then cycle through the even numbers.
- With the whole class, count in unison from 0 to 24 in steps of 2, then count backwards from 24 to 0.
- Randomly challenge children to count on from a number called out. So, if "12 on" is called out they must count 14, 16, 18… up to 24. Once the process is understood, introduce the process for counting back, and call "12 back" to prompt the counting of 10, 8, 6… down to 0.
- Ask the children to draw 2 lines of 12 dots each, 1 above the other, to form an array of 24 dots.
- Now repeat the activity above, using an array of 24 dots (digital file 5) where each click on the first screen reveals 2 dots. Start with any number of dots you choose then ask the children to count on in 2s as each click reveals another pair of dots. So, if you start with 12 dots showing, you can click through to 24 as children count in 2s. Use the second screen for counting back as each click hides 2 dots.
- Randomly call out numbers from the 2-times table, and ask: *If this is the answer, what might the question be?*

EXTEND

Working in small groups, ask the children to play the same game (with no array) by taking turns to say the start number and the direction of the count and testing each other's clarity and precision in counting on and back in 2s.

2-TIMES TABLE: PAIRS TOWER

You need: digital file 6 (Paris tower); cm squared paper; snap cubes (optional)

STEPS

- Explain that there is an apartment block called Pairs Tower. It has that name because there is a pair of apartments on each floor. The lift is broken so the postal worker has to use the stairs. There are no apartments on the ground floor, but there are 2 doors on all the other floors, right up to the 12th floor. So, if the postal worker visits the 2nd floor they will have seen 4 doors in total; if they visit the 8th floor, they will have seen 16 doors in total.
- Display digital file 6 (Paris tower). You can amend the numbers in the table if you wish, or use the ones already shown.

Day	Mon	Tue	Weds	Thu	Fri
Highest floor visited	2	7	4	5	10

- Explain how the table works, for example for Monday the postal worker would have seen 2 doors per floor for 2 floors, giving $2 \times 2 = 4$ doors.
- Working in pairs, challenge the children to state how many doors the postal worker saw on each day, and the total that they saw in the week. To support their calculations, children can use cm squared paper to draw a column 2 squares wide and 12 squares high, or build it with snap cubes.
- Ask: *How might you use the answer from 1 floor to help you with the next floor? What is the quickest way to work out the weekly total?*

EXTEND

Make trickier statements, such as: I start on the 4th floor and go up to the 10th, how many doors do I see? (14) Children will need to think carefully about the number of floors with doors seen.

2-TIMES TABLE: 2's COMPANY

You need: A4 paper and pens

STEPS

- Arrange the children in pairs and explain that they are going to make a worksheet for a Year 2 child to revise and practise their 2-times table, and they each have to create 6 to 8 problems focusing on the 2-times table, such as, "If there are 7 monkeys in a room, how many eyes will there be altogether?" and, "A teacher counts 6 shoes in the cloakroom. How many children are not wearing their shoes?" Discuss the limits of their problems (no greater number than 24; single-step only; child-friendly scenarios; avoid repetition of calculations), and brainstorm contexts and objects that are suitable for the age-range (such as zoos, 2p coins, sweets sold individually, body parts that come in pairs).
- Also, encourage children to make the problems on their worksheet become progressively more difficult, in particular ensuring a reasonable balance between multiplication and division problems.
- Pairs should note their answers separately. They should be given the opportunity to evaluate other groups' worksheets to ensure variation, progression, accuracy and appropriateness. These can then be shared with the Year 2 children.
- Ask: *What did you notice about the numbers and words you used? What was difficult, and what was easy about writing the worksheet?*

EXTEND

Move on to 2-step problems, such as, "I have 3 2p coins in 1 pocket, and 5 in the other. How much money do I have altogether?" Can they adapt/re-write their original problems to make them harder?

3-TIMES TABLE: TRIPLETS

You need: digital file 7 (Triplets); sets of number cards 0–9 (enough for 1 set per 4 children)

STEPS

- Display the 3-times table facts (digital file 7). Looking at the digits in the 1s column of the answers, discuss the 'pattern' for the 1s. (Every digit appears once, and repetition only occurs once we reach 33.)
- Using a pile of number cards from 0–9, turn over the top card. Agree which 3-times table fact this can be used for (for example 6 can be used for $2 \times 3 = 6$; 1 can be used for $7 \times 3 = 21$). Note that 3 and 6 both contribute to 2 facts each ($1 \times 3 = 3$, $11 \times 3 = 33$, and $2 \times 3 = 6$, $12 \times 3 = 36$).
- Arrange the children in small groups, each with a set of 0–9 cards. Explain that they must take it in turns to turn over a card, then state the table fact it contributes to (for example turn over 4: $8 \times 3 = 24$). Children must monitor each other's answers, and work until they have covered the whole of the 3-times table.
- Conclude with random quick-fire questions, calling the answers, with children having to state the times tables fact (for example *33: 11×3*). Ask: *Knowing that fact, can you say the fact above or below it?*

EXTEND

Ask children to work in groups of 4. Give each group 4 small slips of paper with the letters A, B, C, D. Explain that, within each group, each person will pick a letter and then A must recite the 3-times table facts from 1 to 3; B does 4 to 6; C does 7 to 9; and D does 10 to 12. Shuffle the slips of paper then children pick up 1 at random. Working in sequence (A to D) each group recites the 3-times table as fast as possible, monitoring each other's progress.

3-TIMES TABLE: 3's COMPANY

You need: cubes or counters

STEPS

- Explain that children are going to work on a problem in which they investigate how to arrange children into groups of 3. Ask them to imagine there is a class of 36 children, and that their teacher needs help in organising the children for different activities. They must always be arranged in groups of 3, with different groups assigned to different activities.
- Demonstrate, using 12 cubes or counters (1 counter per group of 3 children) how for 2 activities (say art and maths), the teacher has varying options, for example 7 groups could do art and 5 could do maths. Write the calculations that show the organisation: 7 × 3 = 21, and 5 × 3 = 15, and of course 21 + 15 = 36, which means all the children in the class are in a group and all the groups are assigned to 1 of the activities.
- In small groups, ask the children to investigate and tabulate the different groupings for 2 activities, and then for 3 activities. Give each group of children 12 counters or cubes to represent the 12 groups of 3 – this is to encourage thinking in 3s, not 1s.
- Sample layout for organising the children into groups for 2 activities:

Activity 1	Activity 2	Total
3 groups: 3 × 3 = 9	9 groups: 9 × 3 = 27	9 + 27 = 36
4 groups: 4 × 3 = 12	8 groups: 8 × 3 = 24	12 + 24 = 36

- Bring the class back together to consider findings. Look for evidence of logical planning of work as well as correct use of facts. Ask: *What patterns can you see between the groups for each activity?* (they must add up to 12), and: *Is there a way you can use the easier facts to help with harder ones?*

EXTEND

Introduce greater numbers of activities to organise the class into, with 5 or 6 activities maximum.

3-TIMES TABLE: STOOLS-R-US

You need: no resources needed

STEPS

- Explain that a factory manufactures stools. For every stool they need a seat and 3 legs.
- 2 simple activities can then be initiated. These can be done as whole-class activities or with children in groups. In groups, ask them to tabulate the number of seats and legs needed for 1 to 12 stools, for example

Number of stools	Number of seats	Number of legs
1	1	3
2	2	6
3	3	9

- For whole class work, firstly call out how many stools you would like (for example 7). Children must write down how many seats and how may legs they need (for 7 stools, 7 seats and 21 legs are needed).
- Continue this, calling out different numbers, and extend thinking by changing your mind after a pause (for example 4 stools… no, 5; 9 stools… no, make it 8.)
- As an alternative, call out the number of legs you have available, and ask the children to state the number of stools they can make (for example 33 legs would give 11 stools). Look out for children who instantly know the answer rather than calculating it.
- Evaluate children's responses, having them check their work via class discussion. Ask: *How could you use this information to help with building 6-legged tables?*

EXTEND

The problems can be made more complex by setting a price per leg, for example £5, and a price per seat, for example £4. The main activity can be repeated, and to push complexity, investigate how many stools can be made with a budget of £100 to buy seats and legs.

SECTION 2

4-TIMES TABLE: PATTERN SPOTTING

You need: digital file 8 (Pattern spotting); pencils and paper (optional)

STEPS

- Display digital file 8 (Pattern spotting). Note how the 1s columns line up.

  1 × 4 = 4   2 × 4 = 8   3 × 4 = 12   4 × 4 = 16   5 × 4 = 20
  6 × 4 = 24   7 × 4 = 28   8 × 4 = 32   9 × 4 = 36   10 × 4 = 40
  11 × 4 = 44   12 × 4 = 48

- In small groups, challenge the children to examine and explain the pattern, or lack of it, in the 4-times table. Through discussion, elicit that the 4-times table repeats itself with a large pattern 1 × 4 to 5 × 4, then 6 × 4 to 10 × 4, then 11 × 4 and 12 × 4. So, the second 5 facts are the first 5 times table facts, each plus 20.
- Practise counting on and back, in steps of 4, to and from 20.
- Repeat this for 24 to 40.
- Working in pairs, ideally without any visual display, ask the children to practise recalling pattern facts. For example the first person says (or writes down) 3 × 4 = 12; their partner must reply 8 × 4 = 32. 1 × 4 = 4 would elicit a reply of 6 × 4 = 24, and so on.
- Note that this activity does not include 11 and 12 times 4, so be sure to cover these too.
- Ask: *If we know that 3 × 4 = 12, what else do we know?* (8 × 4 = 32). Repeat, using various facts from 1 × 4 to 5 × 4.
- If appropriate, extend this further using the facts from 6 × 4 to 10 × 4.

EXTEND

Repeat the main activity using division facts. So, the first person says 40 ÷ 4 = 10, prompting their partner to say 20 ÷ 4 = 5. Do not move on until both agree to each other's facts.

4-TIMES TABLE: FINGERS AND THUMBS

You need: no resources needed

STEPS

- Organise the class into groups of 6, ideally with each group sitting around a table in a rough circle. Explain that no speaking is allowed; eye contact and some hand movements are the only movements allowed.
- Ask each group to sit with the fingers of both hands placed on the edge of their table (or on laps if no table is available). Their fingers should be straight, and the thumbs free to wiggle up and down.
- Explain that, between them, each group has 12 lots of 4 fingers.
- They must work as a group to display the correct number of hands and fingers for each multiplication fact called out. They must do this by hiding unneeded hands (under the table or behind their back) and keeping other hands visible. They cannot talk or mouth words.
- Start by calling 48 (or 12 × 4 = 48 to make it easier), followed by 0 × 4 = 0 to help establish rules. Repeat this for a range of 4-times table facts, ensuring children work silently but cooperatively to represent the fact correctly.
- To conclude, bring the class together again and discuss strategies and problems, focusing on discussing the individual table's facts. Children should aim to identify whether insecure knowledge hampered them at all.

EXTEND

Back in groups of 6, practise whizzing round the circle to recite the 4-times table. Starting with no hands/fingers visible, then moving, Mexican wave style, to add multiples of 4 as each hand descends. Children should recite the table as this happens, mentally or verbally as a group.

4-TIMES TABLE: ODD ONES OUT

You need: Pencils and paper

STEPS

- Explain that there are 3 'rogue' facts in the 4-times table – the only 3 facts that do not have a 'partner'.
- Working in pairs, explain that they have to find the 3 4-times table facts that do not have 'partners', and try to find out why (a partner being the double or half of 1 other number in the table, for example 2 × 4 has 1 × 4 and 4 × 4 as its partners, and the 3 'rogue' facts are 7 × 4 = 28, 9 × 4 = 36 and 11 × 4 = 44; being odd numbers they do not have a 'half', and their doubles are too big for the 4-times table).
- Ask the children to write out all of the facts from the 4-times table, placing partners next to each other, and placing the 'loners' alone.
- In reviewing and discussing work, draw out discussion on odd and even numbers as appropriate. Ask: *Why do these 3 have no partner?*
- Use rapid questioning to consolidate knowledge of 'partner' facts, stating 1 fact and requesting its partner (for example 3 × 4 = 12 requires the reply 6 × 4 = 24).

EXTEND

Repeat the activity, but writing every fact as a division (for example 48 ÷ 4 = 12, with 'partner' 24 ÷ 4 = 6).

5-TIMES TABLE: GIMME 5

You need: A large space

STEPS

- Quickly review the 5-times table, reviewing the basic pattern it contains.
- Stand 12 children in a circle, and you stand in the middle. Ensuring that all the children are facing the same way, with their right hand raised 'gimme-5' style, walk around the circle clapping the hand of each child. The object is for them to shout out the appropriate multiple of 5.
- Nominate a child to be the first, so they will shout "5", the second child "10", the third "15" and so on, all the way to 60.
- After this, challenge all of the class to state which times tables fact each person represents (for example Chrissy shouted 45 – she is 9 times 5.)
- A variant is to have each child call out their place in the circle when they are clapped (for example 2…) and the rest of the circle chant to complete the times tables fact: …5s are 10!*)*
- Challenge the class to work in groups of 13 and come up with a strategy (including allocated numbers of course) to recite the times tables as quickly as possible. Have races or time trials.
- Gather the class together and discuss strategies, asking children to reflect on what they might still find difficult.
- Consolidate learning playing 'True or False', calling out accurate or inaccurate 5-times table facts (6 × 5 = 30; 9 × 5 = 35; 3 × 5 = 15, etc*)*, hands up only for a 'false' fact.

EXTEND

Reverse the circle, starting with 60 and reducing the count by 5 each time – either counting the multiples or reciting the complete times table facts.

5-TIMES TABLE: TALLY HO!

You need: no resources needed

STEPS

- Revise the use of 5 bar gates in tally charts.
- Draw 12 5 bar gates in a row on the board:

  |||| |||| |||| |||| |||| ||||
  |||| |||| |||| |||| |||| ||||

- Ask the class to count how many lines there are in the first 2 'gates' (10). Discuss the laborious nature of this, and consider how much quicker it is to refer to each bar gate as '5'.
- Next, move along the first few gates, this time counting the 5s: *5, 10, 15…*.
- Working with the whole class, pose questions to them. Ask: *If this was a tally count for cars, and I counted 8 gates worth of cars, how many cars would that be?* Extend this with questions like, *How do you know? What if I saw 1 gate fewer?* and so on.

EXTEND

Introduce division by inverting the questions, for example *How many 'gates' for 55 cars?* and so on.

5-TIMES TABLE: HAND IN GLOVE

You need: no resources needed

STEPS

- Explain that a glove manufacturer uses a very basic technique to make each pair of gloves. They simply join 2 square pieces of fabric together at each side. They leave a bottom hole for the hand to go in, and then sew on 5 identical 'finger holders' at the top – 1 for each finger and 1 for the thumb.
- So, to make 1 glove they need 2 squares of fabric and 5 finger holders.
- Ask: *What will they need to make 4 gloves?* (8 squares of fabric and 20 'finger holders'), always asking the children to explain their answers.
- Continue with random glove quantities using rapid-fire questioning.
- Arranging the class as desired, ask the children to draw a chart for every amount of material needed for 1 to 12 gloves.

Gloves	Squares of cloth	Finger holders
1	2	5
2	4	10

- Note that there is also 2-times table work going on here. Focus on this also if desired.

EXTEND

If the children seem ready, the scope of the problems can be increased by asking them to find far larger quantities, but discussing strategies beforehand, for example to make 60 gloves, first calculate the squares and fingers needed for 10 gloves (20 and 50 respectively) and then multiply each by 6.

Test the 2-, 3-, 4- and 5-times tables

6-TIMES TABLE: PACK OF 6

You need: digital file (Times tables square) for class display; resource 2 (Times tables square)

STEPS

- Use a large times tables square (digital file 1) to revise the 6-times table and discuss any patterns. If appropriate, ask questions to elicit the similarities and differences between the 6-times table and the 2- and 3-times tables. Ask: *Are the 2-times table facts in the 6-times table always, sometimes or never? Are the 3-times table facts in the 6-times table always, sometimes or never? How often do the 2-, 3- and 6-times tables meet up?*
- Ask the class to close their eyes and, in unison, work through the 6-times table, leaving gaps for the answers (for example *1 6 is _____, 2 6s are _____*). Tell the children that they must consider which facts do not come instantly to them. They won't necessarily be able to recall all gaps, but awareness is enough at this stage.
- Next, working in pairs, ask the children to recite the 6-times table from memory, to a partner, with the partner monitoring progress by looking at a times tables square. The partner can note which facts are incorrect or insecure. (Children who are competent can support those who need help.)
- Pairs then move into groups of 4 or 6 to discuss their insecure facts, and consider strategies for how they might remember them (for example 5×6 is half of 10×6, so must be 30; 9×6 is 6 less than 60, so must be 54, and so on).
- Gather the class together and share strategies for remembering the less secure facts. Use the opportunity to note any misconceptions or confusion.

EXTEND

With weaknesses identified, use short, focused sessions to count in multiples of 6, both forward from 0 and backwards from 72.

6-TIMES TABLE: TUMBLING DICE

You need: digital file (Times tables square) for class display; resource 2 (Times tables square); 2 dice per group of 4 children; counters

STEPS

- Display a large times tables square (digital file 1) and quickly revise the 6-times table.
- Roll the 2 dice and show how, by using 1 of the dice, or by adding the totals, a 6-times table fact can be found (for example if a 2 and a 5 are rolled, we can choose the 2 for 2×6, the 5 for 5×6, or add them together for 7×6). Emphasise that only 1 of the 3 facts can be chosen per roll of the 2 dice.
- Working in small groups, the children must 'race' against each other to complete every fact on their 6-times table square, using times tables squares (resource 2), rolling 2 dice each time and selecting which of the 3 available facts they will use then crossing out that number. Emphasise that they must monitor each other's answers.
- Extend learning by asking inverted questions to the whole class, such as *If I said 42, what 2 numbers might I have rolled?* (6 and 1; 3 and 4; or 2 and 5).

EXTEND

Repeat the main game, but the faster version. Children roll 2 dice and quickly state the 2 or 3 6-times table facts that the dice reveals (for example a 1 and a 4 give $1 \times 6 = 6$, $4 \times 6 = 24$, and $5 \times 6 = 30$).

6-TIMES TABLE: HEN POWER

You need: paper; cubes or counters

STEPS

- A farmer organises her hens in groups of 6. In every field she puts a henhouse for every 6 hens in that field.

- Work through an example field. Say that there are 36 hens in the field, so how many henhouses will be needed? (6)
- Ensure that children (either alone, in pairs or in small groups) have a sheet of paper and a supply of small cubes or counters (the cubes or counters represent henhouses).
- Ask the children to divide their paper up into 8 equal sections, and then guide them to write a selection of hen numbers for different fields – all taken from the 6-times table (for example 42, 66, 12, etc), and to write these numbers in each field. Children must then calculate the number of henhouses needed for each field, adding counters to help if needed. Ideally their findings can be presented in tabular form.
- Review children's work and ask questions to extend learning, such as: *How do you know that? What if 6 hens were removed from the field? What if the number of hens were doubled?*
- Consolidate and extend the learning by presenting deliberately incorrect statements for the class to resolve, such as, *A field has 14 hens and 2 henhouses. What has gone wrong?* (Either there are 2 hens too many, or there are 4 too few hens and an extra henhouse is needed.)

EXTEND

Repeat the scenario, but stating numbers of hens per field that are ***not*** from the 6-times table, such as 38. Children must state the number of henhouses needed and how many hens will be left over in each field.

7-TIMES TABLE: KNOWLEDGE BUILDING

You need: digital file (Times tables square) for class display

STEPS

- Explain that the 7-times table can be difficult to learn; as well as having little in common with other times tables, there is no strong pattern to it.
- If desired, use a large times tables square (digital file 1) to spend time focusing on the nature of '7' and its times table: it is a prime number; much like the 3-times table, every digit appears once in the 1s column, and repetition only occurs once we reach 77.
- Tell the class that, together, you will build a structure for learning all of the 7-times table facts.
- Ask: *Of the 12 facts in the 7-times table, which are easy to know?* Hopefully the children will agree that $1 \times 7 = 7$, $10 \times 7 = 70$, and $11 \times 7 = 77$ are all easy.
- Staying with just those facts, ask: *What would 1 7 more make for each fact? What would 1 7 less make for each fact?* This should also elicit $2 \times 7 = 14$, $9 \times 7 = 63$, and $12 \times 7 = 84$.
- Cover the remaining facts, considering strategies for learning each 1. On encountering facts ask: *This is a hard 1 – how might I recall it?*, and consider strategies such as referring to other tables (if we want to know 7×3, try 3×7 – do we know it?), all the while reminding the class to consider the preceding and subsequent fact in the table.
- To conclude, ask: *Can you give me any 7-times table fact? Another, another, another?*

EXTEND

Save counting in multiples for extension work. Rather than pushing children to recall all the facts as quickly as possible, try setting them a slow and steady pace – they may need to continually calculate as they go. If necessary, have the multiples listed in a line for children to look at if they are particularly insecure with this table.

7-TIMES TABLE: GETTING TO KNOW YOU

You need: digital file (Times tables square) for class display; resource 2 (Times tables square)

STEPS

- Display a large times tables square (digital file 1) and look at the 7-times table. With the table visible, count through the multiples of 7, and then ask random facts from this table, allowing the class to locate and read off the answers if necessary.
- With the times tables hidden, repeat the activity, discussing outcomes and difficulties and comparing easier-to-remember facts with harder ones. Say: *Tell me a hard fact from this table. Tell me an easy fact from this table.*
- Now ask the class to consider the other times tables, starting with the 2-times table. Either recalling the 2×7 fact in isolation, or in relation to the nearest-known fact, (for example $5 \times 2 = 10$, so 7×2 is 14). Repeat this for other tables, focusing specifically on 7 as the number to be multiplied in each table.
- Children can now work in pairs to practise facts on each other, noting which facts they are not secure with, and studying the times tables square to help improve their learning.
- Use quick-fire questions to focus on easier facts, such as $10 \times 7 = 70$ and $2 \times 7 = 14$, and ask: *What other 7-times table facts can this help you with? Are there any more?*

EXTEND

The activity can progress to division. Start by listing the multiples of 7, in order, and work through them with 7 as the divisor (for example $35 \div 7 = 5$). For each 1, consider the alternative fact ($35 \div 5 = 7$). Build familiarity with the 7-times table facts, all the while encouraging understanding of the links to other times tables.

7-TIMES TABLE: DEAR DIARY

You need: resource 4 (Jungle supplies)

STEPS

- Set the context: explain that the class has been tasked with providing supplies for people who are going to live in the jungle. Display resource 4 (Jungle supplies) and look through the items on it.
- Explain the task: that 7 people (these could be names of the children's choosing, themselves, celebrities, etc) are entering a survival competition – they are entering the jungle as a group for 7 weeks. They must all survive for the team to win.
- Working in small groups, children must decide on the correct amount of provisions that will be needed for the entire 7 weeks.
- It is advisable to spend some time considering the available resources, reminding the class that some of the quantities will have left-over amounts, and this should be kept to a minimum.
- Note that children will also have to decide on the number of meals, what they will eat for each meal, and so on. Leave this open.
- As an open investigation, encourage children to work collaboratively and imaginatively. Explain that you want them to provide their estimations using multiplication facts; these will be largely, but not entirely, from the 7-times table.

EXTEND

The task can be repeated, but in a slightly different vein, by stipulating that there is a set amount of each item on the list (such as 20 of each item), with the challenge being to calculate what is the longest time 7 people could survive on such a supply. Again, allow for creative solutions, all backed up by clear calculations and recordings.

8-TIMES TABLE: HAVE I SEEN YOU B4?

You need: digital file 9 (Have I seen you B4?); pencils and paper (optional)

STEPS

- Explain that the 8-times table is one of the harder ones to learn. It does, though, have something in common with the 4-times table: it repeats itself with a large pattern. Display digital file 9 (Have I seen you B4?) and use this to explain how the second 5 facts are the first 5 + 40, that is 1 × 8 to 5 × 8, then 6 × 8 to 10 × 8, then 11 and 12 × 8.
- Discuss the pattern, or lack of it, in the table, and practise counting on and back, in steps of 8, to and from 40. Next, repeat this for 48 to 80.
- Move on to reciting the full 8-times table facts from 1 to 5, then 6 to 10.
- Use quick-fire questioning to state a single fact (for example 3 × 8 = 24) and challenge the class to find its 'partner' (8 × 8 = 64).
- Ask the children to work in pairs to learn the 2 'halves' of the 8-times table by relating facts and their partners.
- Note that this activity does not include 11- and 12-times 8, so be sure to cover these too.

EXTEND

- Repeat the main activity using division facts, for example the first person says 32 ÷ 8 = 4, prompting their partner to say 72 ÷ 8 = 9. (The 1s digits match.) Do not move on until both agree to each other's facts.

8-TIMES TABLE: HAPPY CLAPPY

You need: no resources needed

STEPS

- Remind the class that they each have 8 fingers (excluding their thumbs). Holding your hands in front of you slowly bring your hands together until they 'clap'. Explain that this clap is bringing 8 fingers together. Ask the children to copy the clap.
- Next, ask the class to close their eyes and listen for claps, counting 8 (fingers) for each clap.
- Clap once (8); restart, then clap twice (16). Be sure to clap slowly to allow for thinking time. Repeat a few times more, going up to a maximum of 5 claps, and repeating facts regularly.
- Ask if the children are counting in multiples of 8 with each clap, or simply counting the claps and then connecting this to the relevant times tables fact. Discuss which might be the best strategy, bearing in mind that how well children know this times table will probably affect their reasoning.
- Encourage children to progress from counting claps to relating the associated times tables fact – this can be forced by clapping faster, proving that recall is faster than counting in multiples.
- Continue the activity, varying the number of claps throughout the whole times table.

EXTEND

Call out a number from the 8-times table (for example 72) and choose a child to clap the correct number of times (9), with the rest of the class verifying if they are correct.

8-TIMES TABLE: SPIDERAMA

You need: digital file 10 (Spiderama); digital file 11 (Spider legs)

STEPS

- Display digital file 10 (Spiderama). Point out that all spiders have 8 legs, and so we have written a large 8 inside the body.
- Explain the meaning of 'arachnophobia' (fear of spiders), and explain that a young person who has this wants to persuade their parents that they need to act. Telling their parents that there are 3 spiders in their room doesn't sound very dramatic, but saying that there are 24 creepy, hairy, spider legs walking towards them has more impact!
- So, the child wants to keep a legs log. They will count the number of spiders in the house each day then work out how many legs this is.
- Create a chart like the one below, or use digital file 11 (Spider legs) adding as many facts as desired. Challenge the children to copy and complete it. Try doing a week's worth, and ask for total numbers of spiders and legs.

Day	Spiders spotted	Legs
1	6	48
2	3	

- In reviewing work, ask: *Could you use earlier answers to help with later ones? Which facts did you find harder to recall?*

EXTEND

Repeat the above activity, but for larger numbers of spiders between 13 and 24. Demonstrate how, for larger numbers of spiders, the number can be split to enable the use of times tables facts, for example 18 spiders is 2 lots of 9 spiders, which is 72 + 72 = 144 legs).

Test the 5-, 6-, 7- and 8-times tables

9-TIMES TABLE: GET HANDY

You need: no resources needed

STEPS

- Demonstrate the method of using our hands to find 9-times table facts up to 90. Hold the hands together in front of you, palms down.

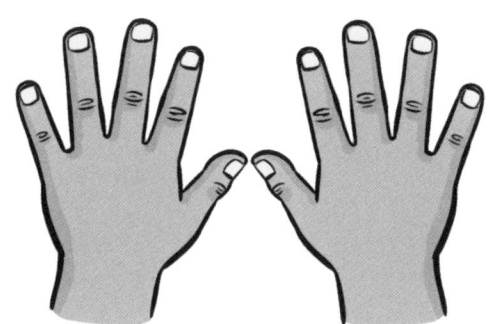

- Show how by dropping a finger, 9-times table facts are revealed. So, dropping the middle finger of the left hand – the third digit along from the left – represents 3 9s. The fingers to the left represent 10s, and those to the right represent 1s.

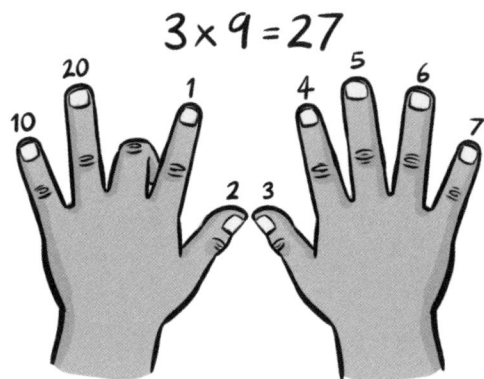

- Give the children time to practise looking at their hands and moving fingers while stating times tables facts from $1 \times 9 = 9$ to $10 \times 9 = 90$.
- Progress to challenging children to recite the 9-times table without looking at their hands (they can still move them under the desk if it helps).
- Conclude by calling out random facts from the table, challenging the class to make each fact with their hand, and to state it followed by 2 other connected facts.

EXTEND

Challenge the children, in pairs, to produce a written or recorded explanation of the method to try on an adult at home. Given that the 'hands' method only works up to 90, be sure to practise recital up to $12 \times 9 = 108$.

SECTION 2

9-TIMES TABLE: POINTERS AND PATTERNS

You need: digital file 12 (Pointers and patterns)

STEPS

- Explain that you are going to learn/review different methods for rapid recall of the 9-times table facts.
- Display digital file 12 (Pointers and patterns) and spend time looking for patterns and, through discussion, elicit that:
  - up to 10×9, the digits in the product always add up to 9 (for example for $9 \times 9 = 81, 8 + 1 = 9$)
  - the 1s decrease by 1 each time, and the 10s increase by 1 each time (9, 18, 27…)
  - the space between 5×9 and 6×9 is like a mirror and the digits in the multiples either side of this 'mirror' are reversed (for example $3 \times 9 = 27$ is the mirror of $8 \times 9 = 72$)
- Children now work in pairs or groups to write sentences that explain their knowledge for example "I know that 2×9 is 18, because the 1 digit of 18 is 1 less than the 2 in 27, and $1 + 8$ is 9." Encourage each group to write approximately 6 statements.
- Bring the class back together and ask groups to challenge each other to complete their statements, stating the first part only, for example "I know that $4 \times 9 = 36$, because…" might elicit a reply of "… it is the mirror of $7 \times 9 = 63$".

EXTEND

Use the totals as a starting point. State a number, such as 27, and ask children to state the calculation.

9-TIMES TABLE: PACKING BOXES

PAGES 12 AND 13

You need: snap cubes (optional)

STEPS

- Explain that boxes of tinned food are packed with 9 tins, arranged in a square. Demonstrate with cubes if required.

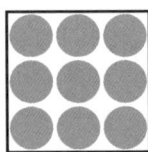

- Tell the children that they are working in a factory which is in charge of packing. Every hour they receive a message on their computer screen telling them how many tins of food have just been produced. They have to calculate how many boxes are needed, and how many tins will be left over. For example 50 tins will require 5 boxes ($5 \times 9 = 45$) with 5 tins left over. 100 tins will require 11 boxes ($11 \times 9 = 99$) with 1 tin left over.
- Arrange the class into appropriate groups and give each group a list of increasingly difficult numbers of tins to plan boxes for. Try to cover most of the 9-times table. Sample lists: easier: 20 tins, 30 tins, 40 tins, 50 tins; harder: 100 tins, 110 tins, 120 tins, 130 tins; difficult: 200 tins, 250 tins, 300 tins, 350 tins.
- To follow up, in discussing answers, talk about how each group made their decisions, discussing the strategies used for identifying the nearest table fact. Ask: *Are there any facts that are harder to recall than others? Why is this? What can you do about it?*

EXTEND

Explain that boxes are stacked in piles of 3 to make carrying easier. Repeat the questions as before, but ask children to keep cumulative totals of the number of boxes generated in each step. The final answer is to provide how many stacks of boxes have been generated. For thoroughness, they can also total the number of left-over tins, and decide how many more 9-tin boxes can be packed.

10-TIMES TABLE: 10 OUT OF 10

You need: digital file (Times tables square) for class display

STEPS

- This activity is worth doing early on when revising times tables with upper Key Stage 2. It gives confidence and sets a benchmark for rapid, fluent recall of multiplication facts.
- Remind the class of the basic operation of counting on from 0, and of counting back to it, in 1s.
- Move on to 10s, clearly counting on in steps of 10, from 0 to 120. Children should be able to do this unaided, but if help is needed display a large times tables square (digital file 1) and use the 10s row or column for support.
- Repeat the activity counting back from 120.
- Children should practise doing this slowly and fluently, progressing to trying to do it as rapidly as possible without becoming unintelligible.
- Finally, in pairs, children could give each other a random multiple of 10 (for example 70) and say 'on' or 'back'. Their partner then has to count on to 120, or back to 0, as clearly and quickly as possible.

EXTEND

Progress to repeated addition of 10s – this is more cumbersome to say, but helps reinforce the concepts involved.

10-TIMES TABLE: SPOT THE GENIUS

You need: no resources needed

STEPS

- Remind the class that numbers can be multiplied in any order ($3 \times 10 = 10 \times 3$), emphasising that for the 10-times table the 10 is last (2×10, 3×10, etc).
- Explain that 0 is not a number, it is a place holder, and when a number is multiplied by 10 its place value increases, with 0 holding the place ($8 \times 10 = 80$ – the 8 has changed from 1s to 10s).
- Stating a range of multiples of 10, (for example 30, 70, 10, 120, 90) challenge the children to identify the calculation that achieved that multiple, emphasising the order from the 10-times table (for example $3 \times 10 = 30$) so that 10 is always the number to be multiplied.
- Allow children to practise this as needed; they should be able to identify calculations instantly.
- Explain that the 10-times table can help you with all the other tables. Ask: *If you know a 10-times fact instantly, what other facts can it help you with?* (The reverse fact, the facts on either side of the 10-times table, etc, for example $8 \times 10 = 80$, so $10 \times 8 = 80$, $9 \times 8 = 72$, and $11 \times 8 = 88$.)

EXTEND

Move on to numbers over 12, repeating the above activity with larger numbers (for example 130, 160, 200, 310, 500, etc).

10-TIMES TABLE: STOCKING UP

PAGES 10 AND 11

You need: resource 5 (Knick-knacks) either for class display or for pairs/group use

STEPS

- Display a large copy of resource 5 (Knick-knacks) and write 10p on the price label on each item.

- Explain that you are a shopkeeper buying new stock and then challenge the class to identify your spending. For example: *I buy 3 bouncy balls and 2 dinosaurs. How much do I spend?*
- For each response ask: *How do you know? Are they right?* and so on.
- Push the level of thinking by explaining that you have £1 or £2 – depending on how complex you want to make the activity – and ask the class to find how much you will have left after 1 or 2 purchases.

EXTEND

The activity can be altered by adding different prices between 2p and 12p to each item, and challenging the class to investigate the cost of buying 'lots of 10', for example How much would 10 dinosaurs, 10 toy cars and 10 bouncy balls cost altogether?

11-TIMES TABLE: RAPIDO!

You need: digital file (Times tables square) for class display

STEPS

- Display a large times tables square (digital file 1) and discuss the 11-times table facts. Discuss how up to 99 the pattern is very straightforward. Ask 1 child to describe what is happening to the numbers (10s and 1s simultaneously increase in single increments).
- Consider how best to recall the facts for 10, 11 and 12, emphasising that they are straightforward but do not continue the pattern of the 1 to 9 facts.
- Next, look at the facts for the 11-times table in relation to the rest of the tables on the times tables square. Ask what children notice and why they think this is. Through discussion, elicit that these facts appear nowhere else as 11 is a prime number.
- Use quick-fire questioning to ask specific tables facts, challenging the children to answer the fact and provide 1 fact lower or higher each time.
- Hide any visible reference to the 11-times table, and practise counting in multiples of 11, keeping a steady speed going throughout. Children should practise this several times to ensure fluent and steady reciting.
- Return to quick-fire questioning, but request that, once the answer is given, counting on in 11s has to continue up to 132 (for example *4 11s? 44… 55, 66, 77, 88…etc*).

EXTEND

Invert the process by stating the answers (for example 121) and asking what the question would be. Then practise counting down the table at speed (for example 121… 110, 99, 88, 77… etc).

11-TIMES TABLE: SAY WHAT YOU MEAN

You need: digital file 4 (Talk proper)

STEPS

- Display digital file 4 (Talk proper) and talk through as many of the terms and definitions as desired.
- Explain that as the 11-times table is reasonably straightforward; it is a useful table to practise vocabulary usage.
- Model explanations of some 11-times table facts using vocabulary from digital file 4 (Talk proper), for example *We can easily calculate 5 × 11, because the number to be multiplied is 11, and as the number 11 is being multiplied by is less than 10 we simply multiply the 10s and 1s separately. 5 × 10 is 50 and 5 × 1 is 5. We know that the sum of 5 and 50 is 55, so we can say that 5 × 11 is 55.*
- Children can then work in pairs to produce 5 sentences that explain different facts (both multiplication and division) from the 11-times table. Challenge them to use as many correct mathematical terms as possible.
- Encourage the class to include information about prime numbers to explain the lack of recurrence of 11-times table facts elsewhere in the tables.

EXTEND

Challenge children to produce explanations for the 3 laws, all based around examples that use the 11-times table as a starting point, for example Associative law: (11 × 3 × 4 = 11 × 12 = 132); Commutative law: (11 × 7 = 7 × 11 = 77); and Distributive law: (11 × (6 + 7) = 11 × 6 + 11 × 7 = 66 + 77 = 143).

11-TIMES TABLE: FOOTBALL CRAZY

You need: digital file 13 (11-times table: Football crazy); resource 6 (Football crazy)

STEPS

- Display digital file 13 (11-times table: Football crazy). This requires some explanation:
  - Each year 12 football teams, who have all scored more goals than they have conceded, are put into 2 lists: 1 for the first half of the season and the other for the second half of the season.
  - For every goal a team has scored more than they have conceded, the difference is multiplied by the number of games they have played (in each case 11). They are then awarded points for that half of the season. (Spend time on the concept and calculation of goal difference; it is the key to the activity.)
  - So, a team that has played 11 games, scored 5 goals and conceded 3, would score 11 × (5 − 3); which is 11 × 2 = 22 points.
  - When the points for each half of the season are added together, the team with the most points is the winner.
- Children should work on completing resource 6 (Football crazy), independently, in pairs or in groups as desired. Once the aim is clear, the process is quite straightforward. Children will succeed if they approach the work methodically.
- The aim is to work out who will get the most points when the points for the 2 halves of the season are added together, and who will get the fewest. (Answer: Team G will get the most with 231 points; and team F will get the fewest with 33 points.)

EXTEND

Ask the children to write out the complete list of teams in order of points, from highest to lowest, and to write how many more points each team scored than the 1 below it. From this, they should write how much better their goal difference was, for example team G won with 231 points, and team L were second with 220 points. There is an 11 point difference, which means that team G had a 1-goal better difference than L.

12-TIMES TABLE: DIFFERENT STROKES

You need: digital file (Times tables square) for class display

STEPS

- Display a large times tables square (digital file 1) and briefly review the 10-times table. The class should be able to rapidly count in multiples of 10.
- Also review the 2-times table. Counting in multiples of 2 should also be secure.
- Look at the first 4 terms on the 12-times table: 12, 24, 36, 48. The 10s increase by 1 each time, the 1s by 2. Point out that these are all straightforward to remember. Spend time practising them both for multiplication and division, using quick-fire questioning.
- Next, show both 5 × 12 = 60 and 10 × 12 = 120 These 2 related facts are also straightforward. Explain that it is the other facts in the 12-times table that are harder to remember/recall.
- Ask the class to consider how they might use the easier-to-remember facts to help them with harder facts. In discussion, try to elicit that doubling is an option (for example 4 × 12 = 48, so 8 × 12 = 96), as is adding lower facts (9 × 12 = 5 × 12 + 4 × 12, which is 60 + 48 = 108).
- Write 12-times table facts from 72 to 108 on the board, 1 at a time, and ask the children to note, then explain, solutions for finding the relevant calculation; not simply to state it.
- Discuss the facts and methods encountered, asking children to consider what works best for them, and what they still feel insecure with. Ask: *How can you help yourself with an insecure fact?* (Consider nearby or related facts, doubles or halves.)

EXTEND

Use the above approach to reinforce the final facts of 11 × 12 and 12 × 12. Ask: *Are methods useful for these 2 facts, or are they better just learned by heart?*

12-TIMES TABLE: EXPLAIN YOURSELF

You need: no resources needed

STEPS

Note: This activity assumes that children are familiar with the way that sections of the 12-times table can be learned separately, as covered in the previous activity, 'Different strokes'.
- Explain that children will be recalling 12-times table facts, explaining 'how they know' after each 1.
- Model expectations with a few statements, such as *1 × 12 = 12. I know this because it is 1 × 10 and 1 × 2. It is a straightforward fact.* and *6 × 12 = 72. I know this because it is 5 × 12 and 1 × 12, which is 60 + 12 = 72.*
- Encourage children to work in small groups to provide a listing of all the 12-times table facts with an explanation of how they know each 1. They should not simply say it is 12 more than the previous fact.
- Explain that the 12-times table overlaps with other tables. Ask: *Is a 12-times table fact always, sometimes or never a 2-/3-/4-/6-/8-times table fact?*

EXTEND

Facilitate cross-class discussion and questioning, asking children to read out their logic for knowing a fact, for example "To find 9 × 12, I take 10 × 12 and subtract 1 12." and then challenge their peers to identify the full fact (9 × 12 = 108). If appropriate, debate whether saying "I just know it." is a good or a bad position to be in (there are pros and cons to each).

12-TIMES TABLE: BAKING BUNS

PAGES 16 AND 17

You need: no resources needed

STEPS

- Explain that the children have been given a temporary job in a bakery, organising the bread buns into bags as they are baked.
- Buns are always put into bags of a dozen. Their job is to take the orders for buns needed and calculate how many bags (dozens) they will need.
- Start by introducing smaller quantities, such as 36 buns (3 bags) and 48 buns (4 bags), moving on to the higher-half of the 12-times table, such as 84 buns (7 bags).
- With the routines well established, arrange the children in pairs or small groups and write a range of bun numbers on the board. These should initially all be from the 12-times table, but can progress to higher multiples of 12. These will require several stages of working and will be trickier.
- Ask children to explain how they could work out the number of bags needed for a number beyond the 12-times table (for example 168). Through discussion, agree that they could subtract 120 (10 × 12) then consider the remainder as a times tables number. So, 168 can be broken down to 10 × 12 = 120 + 4 × 12 = 48, so there will be 14 bags of buns.

EXTEND

Name different bun-bag numbers and challenge the class to find the number of buns in them, starting within the 12-times table then going beyond, for example
15 bags = 144 + 36 = 180 buns.

BINGO!

You need: digital file (Times tables square) for class display; resource 2 (Times tables square); counters/pencils/non-permanent pens

STEPS

- This game can be played more than once.
- Explain that you will be calling out multiplication facts and that the class must cover up each number once they have identified it on their times tables square. Model examples using various terms, such as 5 times 4; 2 3s; 6 lots of 7; and so on.
- Now – the twist compared to ordinary bingo: if the answer to any question appears more than once on the times tables square, children should cover all the squares that contain that number. So, for 4 × 5 = 20, children can mark off 4 squares: 4 × 5 = 20; 5 × 4 = 20; 2 × 10 = 20; and 10 × 2 = 20.
- As soon as anyone identifies 4 squares that are touching each other – in a line, a square or an 'L' shape, they must call "Bingo!" Check with the class that all of those answers are correct; mark those squares as being 'answered'; then continue.
- Difficulty can be altered according to how questions are paced.

EXTEND

Instead of using times tables squares use a 100 square, or better still a 144 square; calling out multiplication facts until 4 numbers that connect in a row (horizontal, vertical or diagonal) are identified.

Test the 9-, 10-, 11- and 12-times tables

TABLE DETECTIVES

You need: digital file (Times tables square) for class display; resource 7 (Who am I?)

STEPS

- This activity is useful as a warm-up during registration, etc. It can be reused regularly, with clues chosen according to the focus number(s).
- Display a large times tables square (digital file 1) and ask the following questions, pausing after each 1 to allow thinking time:
  - I am an odd number
  - I only appear once on the table.
  - I am a square number
  - I am less than 50
  - I am greater than 30
  - What number am I, and how do you make me? (Answer: 49; 7 × 7)
- After each set of questions ask: *How soon did you realise the answer? What stopped you from saying it? How can you be sure?*
- Resource 7 (Who am I?) provides 6 other 'Who am I?' sets of clues. These can either be distributed to the class or read aloud.
- The 6 answers are: 1. 12 (3 × 4); 2. 55 (11 × 5); 3. 48 (6 × 8); 4. 36 (9 × 4 or 3 × 12); 5. 21 (7 × 3); 6. 64 (8 × 8).
- Make some more 'Who am I?' clues, and encourage the children to work in pairs to discuss the clues and whittle down the numbers until they find the correct answer.

EXTEND

Challenge the children to make their own 'Who am I?' clue cards, using appropriate language and correct mathematical terms.

THIS AND THAT

You need: resource 5 (Knick-knacks)

STEPS

- Note that there is a separate Knick-knacks activity for the 10-times table.
- This is an activity that can be easily repeated by changing the values of different items. You can choose whether you focus on 1, a few, or all of the times tables.
- Use a copy of resource 5 (Knick-knacks) and assign a price to each item from 1p to 12p (or £1 to £12 for more realistic prices). Write the prices on the labels.
- Display a large version of the annotated resource 5 (Knick-knacks) or distribute copies, and provide a 'shopping list' of all the items, for example the shopping list might state that 5 of every item is required to fill party bags, or it could be more specific – 3 pencils, 2 erasers and a pencil sharpener.
- Children then have to calculate the cost of each item and the total cost.

EXTEND

The activity is easily extendable by creating greater shopping lists. To add a step, request that children find the change that would be left over from a £20 note.

INVESTIGATING THE TIMES TABLES

3

The times tables are full of hidden relationships and unusual facts. This section provides activities that help to investigate and uncover these aspects of the tables. These investigations provide children with a more secure understanding of the properties of number, and of the tables themselves.

Number walls are used in several of the activities and provide a strong visual image for patterns. You may choose to use number rods to allow children hands-on opportunities to build and explore using number walls.

$9 \times 2 = 18$

$6 \times 3 = 18$

$3 \times 6 = 18$

$2 \times 9 = 18$

Activity	Objective	Focus	Organisation	Development
Pattern spotting (p45)	Recall multiplication and division facts for multiplication tables up to 12 × 12	Considering the pattern created by different number ranges. Examining the location and relationship of number in the 20s, 30s, 40s, etc	Pairs	Reasoning
Links (p45)	Solve problems involving multiplication and division including using their knowledge of factors and multiples, squares and cubes	Exploring recurring numbers on the times tables square. Explaining what recurring numbers have in common.	Whole class	Reasoning
Odds and evens (p46)	Recall multiplication and division facts for multiplication tables up to 12 × 12	Understanding the distribution of odd and even numbers in the tables. Looking at why there are 3 times as many even numbers as odd numbers.	Whole class	Reasoning

Activity	Objective	Focus	Organisation	Development
Number wall 1: building blocks (p46)	Recall multiplication and division facts for multiplication tables up to 12 × 12; identify multiples and factors, including finding all factor pairs of a number, and common factors of 2 numbers	Understanding why some tables have common links. Investigating how the 2-, 5- and 10-times tables relate.	Small groups	Reasoning
Number wall 2: triplets (p47)		Understanding why some tables have common links. Investigating how the 3-, 6- and 9-times tables relate.	Small groups	Reasoning
Number wall 3: going further (p47)		Understanding why some tables have common links. Investigating how the times tables continue beyond multiples of 12.	Whole class	Reasoning
The factors of life (p48)	Identify multiples and factors, including finding all factor pairs of a number, and common factors of 2 numbers	To develop understanding and use of factors. Finding factors for recurring numbers in the times tables.	Whole class, pairs for extension	Reasoning
Working with multiples (p48)	Identify multiples and factors, including finding all factor pairs of a number, and common factors of 2 numbers; count in multiples	To develop understanding and use of multiples. Considering strategies for identifying multiples.	Small groups	Reasoning
Prime time (p49)	Know and use the vocabulary of prime numbers, prime factors and composite (non-prime) numbers; establish whether a number up to 100 is prime and recall prime numbers up to 19	Understand the role of prime numbers in the times tables. Investigating the times tables facts that have prime factor pairs.	Whole class	Reasoning
Square tables (p49)	Recognise and use square numbers and the notation for squared (^{2})	Understanding the role of square numbers in the times tables. Using knowledge of square numbers to support times tables learning.	Whole class	Reasoning

Assessment

This section has covered the patterns of the times tables, requiring both the application of table facts as well as a greater understanding of how numbers inter-relate, and the properties of individual numbers. Questions to help assess this deeper understanding might include the following:

- *Why does the number 12 occur several times in the times tables?*
- *Why does the number 25 only occur once?*
- *Why is 31 not in the times tables at all?*
- *Why is only a quarter of the times tables odd numbers?*
- *An even number that is divisible by 3 is also divisible by 6. Is this always, sometimes or never true?*
- *What times tables facts link to $1 \times 12 = 12$ (or $1 \times 9 = 9$, $2 \times 10 = 20$, etc)?*
- *What are the common multiples of the 4 and 5 times tables?* (This can work with any 2 tables.)
- *What factors do 42 and 21 have in common?* (This can work with any 2 or more numbers.)

PATTERN SPOTTING

You need: digital file 14 (Pattern spotting) for class display; resource 2 (Times tables square)

STEPS

- Display digital file 14 (Pattern spotting) and show slide 1, which shows all of the square numbers highlighted (1, 4, 9, 16, etc). Click to slide 2 to show every number between 10 and 19 which lies below the diagonal highlighted. Finally click again to show slide 3, which shows every number between 10 and 19 above the diagonal highlighted.

×	1	2	3	4	5	6	7	8	9	10	11	12
1	1	2	3	4	5	6	7	8	9	10	11	12
2	2	4	6	8	10	12	14	16	18	20	22	24
3	3	6	9	12	15	18	21	24	27	30	33	36
4	4	8	12	16	20	24	28	32	36	40	44	48
5	5	10	15	20	25	30	35	40	45	50	55	60
6	6	12	18	24	30	36	42	48	54	60	66	72
7	7	14	21	28	35	42	49	56	63	70	77	84
8	8	16	24	32	40	48	56	64	72	80	88	96
9	9	18	27	36	45	54	63	72	81	90	99	108
10	10	20	30	40	50	60	70	80	90	100	110	120
11	11	22	33	44	55	66	77	88	99	110	121	132
12	12	24	36	48	60	72	84	96	108	120	132	144

- Discuss the reflective symmetry of the pattern (starting with 10, 11, 12 and noting how this relates to the numbers next to them, then move onto the columns in the 2- and 3-times tables).
- Distribute times tables square (resource 2) and challenge the children, in pairs, to investigate the numbers from 20–29, 30–39, etc. Ask what they can deduce about the items in each range, and their relationship to the reflected facts. (There are more numbers in the 10s than the 20s, the numbers in each range steadily reduce until there are only 2 numbers in each range over 100.) The columns on the left-hand side reflect to rows on the right-hand side, with individual facts being the reverse multiplication (so the commutative law is illustrated: 4 × 5 = 20, and 5 × 4 = 20).
- Ask: *Which number range (1–9; 10–19; 20–29; 30–39, etc) has the greatest number of multiples on the table? Why is this?* (10–19, because smaller factors mean more numbers that are on the times tables square are made.)

EXTEND

The times tables go up to 144. 72 is half of 144. How many of the numbers on the times tables square are less than 72? How many are more than 72? Does this seem logical?

LINKS

You need: digital file (Times tables square) for class display; resource 2 (Times tables square)

STEPS

- Display a large times tables square (digital file 1) and ask the class to find a number that occurs 6 times (12 and 24). Circle every instance of 12 in 1 colour, and 24 in another colour.
- Repeat this for the numbers that occur 4 times (6, 8, 10, 18, 20, 30, 40, 48, 60, 72).
- Choosing 1 of the above numbers (for example 12), work as a class to investigate why it reoccurs, guiding the children towards discussing the commutative law (6 × 2 = 2 × 6), common multiples, and factor pairs (1 and 12, 2 and 6, 3 and 4).
- Keeping the focus on 12, reinforce which pairs 'partner' each other, emphasising the commutative law as above.
- Ask: *Why, if the times tables go up to 144, are 12 and 24 the most recurring numbers? Why not a higher number?* (This is because higher numbers, such as 48 and 96, do have more factors than 12 and 24, but many of these are not on the times tables square, for example 2 × 24.)
- Challenge the class to find every number greater than 40 that appears **more than** twice on the square. They should investigate and explain these occurrences (40, 48, 60 and 72).
- Ask: *What knowledge can you use to assess if a number will appear frequently in the tables?* (number of factors)

EXTEND

Challenge the class to investigate the occurrence of 36, and to explain why it appears an odd number of times (5).

INVESTIGATING THE TIMES TABLES: PATTERNS, LINKS AND PROPERTIES OF NUMBERS

SECTION 3

ODDS AND EVENS

You need: digital file 15 (Odds and evens) for class display; resource 2 (Times tables square)

STEPS

- Display digital file 15 (Odds and evens), discussing the pattern which is formed.
- Distribute times tables squares (resource 2) to each child and, as a class, work to identify all of the odd numbers in the times tables square, discussing why every other row has no odd numbers at all.
- Explain that there are 144 numbers on the square, and that 36 of them are odd. Ask what proportion this is (1 in 4).
- Work together to identify the rules that dictate whether a times tables fact will be odd (the numbers to be multiplied must both be odd).
- Practise recalling odd times tables facts, using questioning such as: *Give me an odd-number table fact with an answer between 20 and 30; and another, and another.*
- Practise spotting the table by asking which table each odd times tables fact belongs to, for example *What table is 77 from? How do you know? What about 21? How do you know?*

EXTEND

Ask the children to explain why there are only 3 odd numbers higher than 80 in the times tables square: 81, 99 and 121. (This is because all other odd numbers between 80 and 144 are either prime numbers and so are not on the times tables square (83, 89, 97, 101, etc) or do not fit into their table as the fact is beyond the twelfth multiple – such as $13 \times 7 = 91$.)

NUMBER WALL 1: BUILDING BLOCKS

You need: digital file 16 (Number wall building blocks); resource 8a (Number wall 1); number rods (optional)

STEPS

- Display the number wall on digital file 16 (Number wall building blocks).

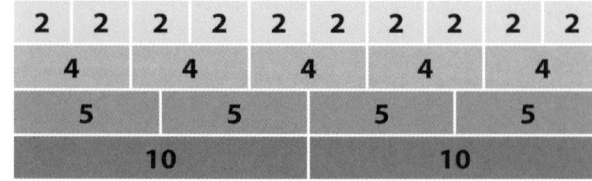

- Ask for times tables facts that the wall illustrates, for example $2 \times 5 = 10$.
- In discussion, list that 10 can be made from 5 2s, 2 5s, or 1 10 (it can also be made from 10 1s of course, although this is not shown on this wall).
- Ask: *Any number that is divisible by 4 is also divisible by 2. Is this always, sometimes or never true?* (always) *Does the same apply to 10 and 5?* (yes) *What would you say about 5 and 2?* (sometimes – every other time) *What about 10 and 4?* (the same)
- In discussion elicit a series of equivalent facts: $10 \times 2 = 5 \times 4 = 4 \times 5 = 2 \times 10$. (If children need support, they can recreate the wall using number rods.)
- Distribute resource 8a (Number wall 1) and ask the children to work in small groups to investigate how they might use the walls to help them calculate beyond the scope of the tables, such as how many 2s are there in 4 10s? For example: *We know that there are 5 2s in 10, so in 4 10s there must be 4 lots of 5 2s, or 20 2s.* In their investigation, encourage children to cut out the blank wall on resource 8d (Blank number wall) and to use numbers and colour (and number rods if preferred) in any way that might support their thinking. They can also join walls to others to extend them.

EXTEND

Ask children if they can devise a method, or formula, for calculating the number of 2s in any number of 10s.

NUMBER WALL 2: TRIPLETS

You need: digital file 17 (Number wall 2 triplets) for class display; resource 8b (Number wall 2); number rods (optional)

STEPS

- Display digital file 17 (Number wall 2 triplets).

2	2	2	2	2	2	2	2	2
3	3	3	3	3	3			
6		6		6				
9				9				

- Ask for some of the times tables facts that the wall illustrates, for example 3 2s equal 6 and 2 3s equal 6.
- Consider how the wall illustrates 'partner facts', for example 2 × 3 is 6, and 3 × 2 is 6.
- Ask: *Why are 9 and 18 divisible by 3, but both are not divisible by 6? Is this the case for all multiples of 9?*
- Work together to write down the 3 ways to make 9: 1 × 9, 3 × 3, 9 × 1; and the 4 ways that the wall shows us how to make 18: 9 × 2, 6 × 3, 3 × 6, 2 × 9.
- Distribute resource 8b (Number wall 2) and challenge the class to work in small groups to use their walls to deduce all of the times tables facts for multiples of 9, including facts beyond the tables (for example 45 2s is 90). Children who need support can use a blank number wall or number rods.

EXTEND

Can children find a rule that allows them to know whether a multiple of 9 will be divisible by 2, 3 or 6? (If it is divisible by 6 (for example 54) it will also be divisible by 2 and 3; if it is even it will always be divisible by 2; if it is odd it will only, and always, be divisible by 3.)

NUMBER WALL 3: GOING FURTHER

PAGES 24 AND 25

You need: digital file 18 (Number wall 3 going further) for class display; resource 8c (Number wall 3); number rods (optional)

STEPS

- Display digital file 18 (Number wall 3 going further).

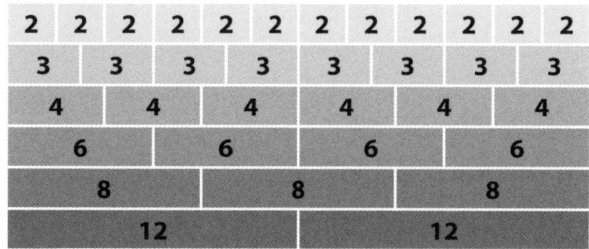

- Ask for some of the times tables facts that the wall illustrates, (for example 3 × 4 = 12, 12 × 2 = 24, 2 × 6 = 12) pushing each respondent to identify 1 or 2 extra facts.
- How many equivalent facts can children find on this wall? Give them a hint, if necessary, that there are 6 ways to make 24, all shown in this wall, but fewer ways to make 12. Ask: *Why is this?* (In fact 12 and 24 can both be made in 6 ways using times tables facts but as the wall does not have 1s on it, 12 × 1 is not available.)
- Explain that if every 12 contains 2 6s, then we can say that 2 12s contain 4 6s, and that 10 12s must contain 20 6s.
- Similarly, if 1 12 contains 3 4s, 10 12s contains 30 4s.
- In discussion elicit that 10 12s must contain 40 3s, and 60 2s!
- Ask: *If 2 12s contains 3 8s, how many 8s will there be in 4 12s?* (6 8s); *What about 10 12s?* (15 8s)
- Distribute resource 8c (Number wall 3) and ask small groups to investigate the number of 2s, 3s, 4s, 6s, 8s and 12s in 60. Ask: *How can you use the number walls to help you? How can you use your knowledge of factors and multiples to help you?* Children who need support can use a blank number wall (resource 8d) or number rods.

EXTEND

Find how many 2s, 3s, 4s, 6s and 8s are in 144.

SECTION 3

THE FACTORS OF LIFE

You need: digital file (Times tables square) for class display

STEPS

- Display a large times tables square (digital file 1) and, together, identify a recurring number on the square (for example 20).
- Ask children to tell you all the facts that make 20 (2 × 10; 4 × 5; 5 × 4; 10 × 2), checking that children are familiar with the commutative law (a × b = b × a).
- Explain the definition of a factor – any number that divides *into* another number with no remainder – and list the factors for 20: 1, 2, 4, 5, 10, 20. Discuss why 1 and 20 do not appear in the list of times tables facts above (1 × 20 is not in the times tables up to 12 × 12 so this fact is not in the times tables square).
- Establish that any times tables fact has at least 2 factors – it is the product of these 2 numbers – and that numbers with more than 2 factors will appear on the times tables square more than once.
- Now work in reverse. Hide the times tables square and write 12 on the board. Ask children to tell you all of its factors (1, 2, 3, 4, 6, 12).
- Looking only at the factors, discuss and then make a list of all of the times tables facts that they provide for us (for example 2 × 6 = 12, 4 × 3 = 12, etc)
- Explain the term 'factor pairs' and demonstrate that every times tables fact is made by a factor pair.
- Ask for a factor pair from the 10-times table. Ask: *Can you give me 1 more? And another? And another?*
- Repeat this as desired for your chosen tables.

EXTEND

List a selection of larger numbers on the board (for example 48, 60, 72). Challenge children to work in pairs to list every factor for each number, and then to write which times tables facts these factors can provide us with.

WORKING WITH MULTIPLES

PAGES 26 AND 27

You need: resource 2 (Times tables square)

STEPS

- Remind the class of the meaning of factors, and explain that a multiple is the reverse of this – a number which can be divided *by* another number with no remainder, for example 15 is a multiple of 5.
- In discussion, elicit that 15 must also be a multiple of 1, 3, and 15; and, just like factors, we can use multiples to deduce times tables facts.
- Choose a number from 1 to 12 (for example 6) and ask: *Which multiples of this number do you know?* Ask for another, and another.
- Point out that by counting in multiples the whole table can be covered (6, 12, 18, 24…72).
- Repeat the above points for different factors as desired.
- Using individual times tables squares (resource 2) and working in small groups, the children discuss and then list common multiples. Explain that these are multiples that several numbers have in common. If they have already done work on factors this should be straightforward for them.
- Gather together and discuss findings, using the opportunity to model good language and vocabulary, requesting that findings are always given in the format "8 is a common multiple of 1, 2, 4 and 8".
- Ask: *If 10 is a multiple of 1, 2, 5 and 10, will all the multiples of 10 also be multiples of these numbers?* (yes)

EXTEND

Using any of the number walls from resource 8, challenge the children to use the walls to make statements about common multiples.

PRIME TIME

You need: digital file (Times tables square) for class display; resource 2 (Times tables square)

STEPS

- Display a large times tables square (digital file 1) and ask: *How many prime numbers are there on this square?*
- As facts are contributed, circle 2, 3, 5, 7, 11 (depending on knowledge and familiarity, this may require further teaching).
- Ask what the class notice about these numbers (they only have themselves and 1 as a factor).
- In discussion, ask the children to list all of the times tables facts that have 2 prime numbers as the factors. Remind children that we call these numbers prime factors, for example $5 \times 7 = 35$, and of course $7 \times 5 = 35$. Ask children to list how often each fact occurs (twice).
- Note that when 1 of the prime factors is 2 there will be some recurring numbers (for example $2 \times 3 = 6$, and $6 \times 1 = 6$). Ask: *Why does this only happen for 2?* (It is because 2 multiplied by 3 and by 5 has a product that is also a times tables factor: $2 \times 3 = 6$, $2 \times 5 = 10$, but for the next smallest primes ($3 \times 5 = 15$), the product is not a times tables factor.)
- For other pairs of factor primes ask: *Why do these numbers only occur twice? Are these numbers harder or easier to remember? Can you use any other facts to help learn them?*

EXTEND

Ask the children to list every times tables fact that is a multiple of a prime number *and* does not occur more than twice. Ask: *Why don't any of the multiples of 7 and 11 occur in any other times tables?* (Because their nearest multiples (14 and 22) are greater than 12 so cannot be factors within the times tables square) and *Why do some of the multiples of 3 and 5 occur in some other times tables?* (Because 6, 9 and 12 are all multiples of 3, and 10 is a multiple of 5.)

SQUARE TABLES

PAGES 28 AND 29

You need: digital file (Times tables square) for class display; digital file 19 (Square tables); resource 2 (Times tables square); cm squared paper

STEPS

- Use digital file 19 (Square tables) to demonstrate how a 1×1 square gives 1 square and a 2×2 square gives 4 squares.

- Display a large times tables square (digital file 1) and look for the facts $1 \times 1 = 1$ and $2 \times 2 = 4$ on it. Ask children what they notice about the locations. (They are all along the diagonal.)
- Introduce the squared notation (for example $5^2 = 25$).
- Highlight the diagonal on the times tables square, reminding the class that this works as a mirror line, and discuss the other square numbers along it. Emphasise to the class that knowing these squares is very useful.
- Ask the class: *Can a square number be a prime number?* (No, it is divisible by the number that was squared.)
- Use repeated questioning to reinforce learning of the square numbers, such as: *If this is the answer, what is the number being squared? Which are the easy squares, which are the hard ones? Can you give me a squared number fact and 2 nearby facts – 1 higher, 1 lower?*
- Progress to challenging children to state all the squares, 1 after another, in ascending then descending order.

EXTEND

Challenge the children to use the square numbers on the times tables square to assist them in learning the facts either side of them, for example "I know that $7 \times 7 = 49$, so 6×7 must be 42, and 8×7 is 56". Assess this with quick-fire questioning, pushing children's thinking with questions such as: *8 9s is tricky, how can you use the square numbers to help you?* ($9 \times 9 = 81$, so $8 \times 9 = 72$).

4
EXTENDING AND APPLYING THE TABLES

This final section provides ideas and activities to help develop children's times table knowledge in various contexts, all from the upper Key Stage 2 mathematics curriculum. Introduced carefully, these activities will help cement children's understanding while allowing them to see the inter-connectedness of different mathematical strands. They are recommended for use once children have become secure in their understanding and use of all 12 of the times tables.

Continue to use concrete resources such as snap cubes and counters to support understanding as well as encouraging the representation of problems visually with rough sketches and bar models.

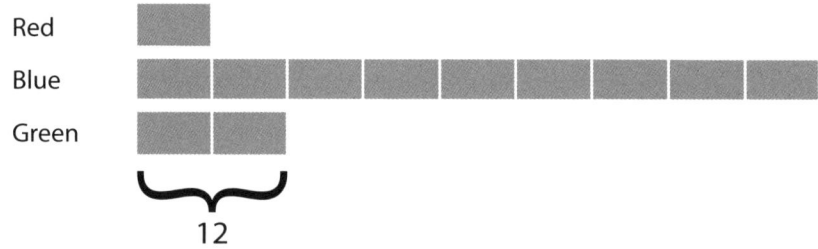

Bar model to show how many red marbles, blue marbles and green marbles in a bag. If the ratio is 1 : 9 : 2 and you know you have 12 green marbles, the number of blue and red marbles can be calculated using 6-times tables facts.

Activity	Objective	Focus	Organisation	Development
Mega-tables: powers of 10 (p53)	Recall multiplication and division facts for multiplication tables up to 12 × 12; multiplying and dividing by powers of 10	Using times tables facts with powers of 10 to perform larger mental calculations. Creating a 'mega-table'.	Pairs	Reasoning
Think big (p53)	Recall multiplication and division facts for multiplication tables up to 12 × 12; multiplying and dividing by powers of 10; solve problems involving multiplication and division	Developing understanding of multiplying powers of 10. Applying times tables skills and powers of 10 knowledge to solve larger problems.	Independent	Problem-solving
Mind control (p54)	Recall multiplication and division facts for multiplication tables up to 12 × 12; solve problems involving multiplying and adding, including using the distributive law to multiply 2 2-digit numbers mentally	Developing competence in multiplying 2 2-digit numbers mentally using times tables facts. Organised approaches to long multiplication.	Independent	Problem-solving

Activity	Objective	Focus	Organisation	Development
Multiplying 2-digit numbers (p54)	Recall multiplication and division facts for multiplication tables up to 12 × 12; solve problems involving multiplying and adding, including using the distributive law to multiply 2-digit numbers by 1 digit	Developing understanding of mental methods in larger calculations. Practising mental methods for multiplying numbers larger than 12 by a single digit.	Pairs or small groups	Reasoning
Scale (p55)	Solve problems involving multiplication and division, including scaling	Calculating scale using only the times tables. Understanding scale.	Whole class	Reasoning
Who shrunk teacher? (p55)	Recall multiplication and division facts for multiplication tables up to 12 × 12; solve problems involving multiplication and division, including scaling	Practising applying more complex numbers to scale reduction problems. Using times tables facts to aid larger calculations.	Independent or pairs	Problem-solving
Losing yer marbles! (p56)	Solve problems involving unequal sharing and grouping using knowledge of fractions and multiples	Applying ratios. Finding numbers of objects to given ratios.	Independent or pairs	Problem-solving
A certain ratio (p56)	Solve problems involving the relative sizes of 2 quantities where missing values can be found by using integer multiplication and division facts	Looking at ratios using only the times tables. Investigating bead ratios.	Groups	Reasoning
Mind your Ps and Qs (p57)	Express missing number problems algebraically; find pairs of numbers that satisfy an equation with 2 unknowns; enumerate possibilities of combinations of 2 variables	Looking at algebra using only the times tables.	Pairs	Reasoning
abc (p57)		Investigating using 3 numbers to make times tables facts. Solving algebraic statements with 3 variables.	Pairs or groups	Problem-solving
Kerching! (p58)	Solve problems in contexts, deciding which operations and methods to use and why	Developing the application of times tables facts to efficient problem-solving. Identifying times tables facts in money problems.	Independent or pairs	Reasoning
Think! (p58)		Solving problems in context. Using extended times tables skills.	Pairs	Problem-solving
1 small step, 1 giant leap (p59)		Looking at multi-step problems involving times tables facts. Identifying and ordering correct steps. (Note: This activity assumes some knowledge of decimals and measures.)	Independent, pairs or small groups as desired	Reasoning
What's what? (p59)		Using times tables facts to solve multi-step problems.	Independent	Problem-solving

EXTENDING AND APPLYING THE TABLES: USING THE TABLES ACROSS THE CURRICULUM

Assessment

This section has covered the use and application of times tables facts to answer questions in other mathematical contexts as well as multiplying larger numbers. Questions to help assess this deeper understanding might include the following:

- *How can times tables facts help you with multiplying by multiples of 10 and 100, such as 20×40, or 7×2000?*
- *Do you have a secure mental method for multiplying larger 2-digit numbers, such as 7×23, or 21×45? Where is your limit?*
  Can you use the same method for multiplying 1-digit × 3-digit numbers? 1-digit × 4-digit numbers? More?
- *Can you use times tables facts to help you with scale problems, such as a 5 : 1 enlargement, or a diagram scale of 1 : 12? Give me an example.*
- *Can you use times tables facts to help you with ratio, such as a ratio of 1 : 3 for boys : girls? If there are 8 boys, how many girls are there?*
- *Can you calculate the value of letters in equations, such as $5d = 45$ ($d = 9$) or $ab = 8$ (multiple values for ab: 1 and 8, 2 and 4, 4 and 2, 8 and 1)?*
- *Can you apply your times tables knowledge to multi-step practical problems, such as money, mass, length? Can you list and explain the steps of calculation you need? Give me an example.*

MEGA-TABLES: POWERS OF 10

You need: no resources needed

STEPS

- Remind the class of the meaning of a power of 10.
- Work through a range of calculations, such as 6 × 10, 6 × 100, 6 × 1000, 6 × 10,000 and discuss the changes in place value, reminding the class that, in these cases, the '0' acts as a place holder. Repeat this activity with other numbers from 1 to 12.
- Progress to considering 'mega-table' facts, such as 3 × 40 = 120, 30 × 40 = 1200, etc.
- Depending on children's previous knowledge and experience, you may have to spend more time clarifying the mathematics behind these calculations (for example 30 × 40 is 3 × 10 × 4 × 10, which is 12 × 100) – note that there are activities designed to explain the associative and commutative laws earlier in this book.
- Working with a partner, challenge the children to create a mega-table of their choice (such as the 5-times table), where every number has been multiplied by 10, for example 40 × 5; 50 × 5; 60 × 5… 120 × 5; 130 × 5, etc)
- Discuss findings and then reinforce new learning with quick-fire mega-questions, such as 30 × 60 (1800); 20 × 70 (1400); and so on. Ask: *How did you do that in your head? Will it be harder for numbers over 100?* (for example 110 × 40 = 4400)
- To push the learning further, give the answers and ask for the questions, such as 4200 (70 × 60), 900 (30 × 30), or 7000 (100 × 70) Ask: *What mental strategy are you using to do these calculations?*

EXTEND

Increase the powers of 10, such as 300 × 20; 500 × 600, or even 8000 × 4000 (this will take them into the millions). Ask: *What is the largest mental calculation you can do that you're sure is right?*

THINK BIG

You need: resource 10 (Think big!)

STEPS

- Recap the operation of multiplying a single-digit number by a power of 10, using quick-fire questions such as 8 × 10, 4 × 100, 1000 × 3, and so on.
- Progress to trickier calculations all within the bounds of the 12-times table, such as 30 × 50 (= 1500), 90 × 40 (= 3600), 80 × 80 (= 1600), and so on. Ask: *How are you using times tables facts to make these calculations easier? How do you know what power of 10 your answer will be? Can you use your answer to find another mega-fact?*
- Distribute resource 10 (Think big!), and ask the children to work though an appropriate section, ensuring the word problems are tackled last of all.
- It is suggested that the 3 sections are worked through separately to consolidate understanding and to pace the learning appropriately. (Note that the answers are not provided – these will need to be agreed between you and the class.)
- Ask: *What is hard about these larger calculations? How can you ensure you don't make mistakes?*

EXTEND

Move on to division problems within the same parameters. (To get you started, invert the questions from resource 10 (Think big!) to create appropriate problems (for example 600 ÷ 30 =___), adapting the numbers as you see fit). It is suggested that only 1 problem is presented at a time for whole-class work, and then individuals may be presented with challenges as appropriate.

MIND CONTROL

You need: resource 11 (Mind control)

STEPS

■ Note that this activity is only appropriate for children who have an understanding and experience of long multiplication when multiplying 2 2-digit numbers together.

■ Write a simple long multiplication on the board, such as 15 × 23, and work through the written method familiar to the class, for example

```
      2 3
  ×   1 5
  ─────────
    1 1 5
    2 3 0
  ─────────
    3 4 5
```

■ Explain that the challenge of this activity is to try and do calculations like this mentally, working though the stages of how to break the calculation down into easier mental chunks, for example 15 × 23 = 10 × 23 + 5 × 20 + 5 × 3, which is 230 + 100 + 15 = 345.

■ Distribute resource 11 (Mind control). Ask children to work through each of the 3 sections separately to consolidate understanding and to pace the learning appropriately. (Note that the answers are not provided – these will need to be agreed between you and the class.)

■ Reassure the children that holding all of this in their head is hard, and is not expected of them. However, it is interesting to see how far we can take our mental abilities. Explain that children should write out the first stage of the calculation – the initial breaking-down – as in the example.

■ After each section, gather the class together and discuss answers. Ask: *What is the trickiest thing about these calculations?* Discussion should reveal that staying organised and focused is the main difficulty. Ask: *How can you overcome this? How can you double check that you have planned properly?*

■ For pure mental calculation, many children will find that there is simply too much to remember. For those who can manage the method with notes, encourage on-going practice using 2-digit numbers that have both digits lower than 6 (for example 31 × 24).

EXTEND

Challenge the class to find the largest possible 2-digit × 2-digit calculation they can manage as a mental calculation.

MULTIPLYING 2-DIGIT NUMBERS

You need: digital file (100 square); resource 9 (100 square); Number cards 2–9

STEPS

■ Warm-up with some easy quick-fire times tables questions from all the tables up to 12 × 12.

■ Ask: *If 4 × 12 = 48, how can we work out what 4 × 13 is?* Explain that, as we know that 4 × 12 = 12 × 4 = 48, then 13 × 4 must be 1 lot of 4 more, so 13 × 4 = 52.

■ Point out, using the distributive law, that 4 × 13 = 4 × 10 + 4 × 3, and that this is 40 + 12 = 52. Emphasise that it is the distributive law which is the key to making the calculations of this session easier.

■ With this in mind, present further calculations, gradually increasing the difficulty level, such as 3 × 14, 5 × 18, 4 × 23, 8 × 62, 39 × 3, etc and work, as a class, through each calculation in turn. Once the 2-digit number is above 20, recap also on multiplying by powers of 10 with times tables facts (for example 4 × 23 = 4 × 20 + 4 × 3, which is 80 + 12 = 92).

■ Once a secure understanding is reached, arrange the children into pairs or small groups and give each group a 100 square (resource 9) and number cards from 2 to 9. Explain that they must take turns to choose a number card (randomly) and to choose a number from the 100 square (again, randomly), then make a calculation. For example they might pick up a 6 card, and with their eyes shut place their finger on 72. So, the calculation would be 6 × 72, or 6 × 70 + 6 × 2, giving 420 + 12 = 432.

■ Share findings. Ask: *Which calculations proved harder to do mentally? Did you come up with any methods to help you?*

EXTEND

Repeat the activity, but focus on the numbers 10, 11, 12. So, children use a 100 square and just these 3 number cards.

SCALE

You need: digital file 21 (Scale)

STEPS

- Explain the format used for scale, demonstrating that 1 : 25 works from small to large, such as the scale of a map or a model of an object. For example a model of 8cm made at a scale of 1 : 25 would represent a real-life object of 8 × 25 = 200cm.
- Display digital file 21 (Scale) and highlight the heights of 5, 6, 7, 8 and 9cm on each figure.
- Choosing the 5cm figure, ask: *If this were a 1 : 20 scale model of a person, what would the actual person's height be?* (5 × 20 = 100cm). Elicit the answer and discuss the process and calculation involved.
- Next, with all of the 5 figures displayed, write a scale of 1 : 12 on the board. In discussion, write the actual height of a person that each model would represent (for example 5cm would represent 5 × 12 = 60cm, a rather tiny person). Repeat this for all 5 figures.
- Finally, stating a larger scale (such as 1 : 25), randomly call out a range of the actual heights these models would be (they will be 125cm, 150cm, 175cm, 200cm and 225cm for 1 : 25). Ask the class to reason which model each of these heights relates to and to verify the answers.

EXTEND

Challenge the class to investigate what actual heights the 5 figures would represent for a range of scales, such as 1 : 20; 1 : 30, 1 : 45, depending on difficulty level required. Ask: *Can you explain a method for finding other heights once you have calculated the first 1?*

WHO SHRUNK TEACHER?

You need: resource 12a (Scale: Who shrunk teacher?); digital file 22 (Who shrunk teacher?)

STEPS

- Recap the main facts of calculating scale.
- Set the scene for this activity, explaining that all of the teachers in a school for magic have been selected for shrinking. Different pupils in this school each have their own specialist un-shrinking scale, so they have been assigned to the teacher who needs them most.
- Distribute resource 12a (Scale: Who shrunk teacher?). Read through the details and then look at the first column – the pupil Amy has been assigned to un-shrink Mr A, and Amy's specialist scale is 1 : 20 – for every 1cm of teacher she can enlarge to 20cm.
- So, Mr A has been shrunk to 9cm, therefore his enlarged height will be 9 × 20cm = 180cm.
- The children can now calculate what the restored height of each teacher will be. Remind them that use of times tables facts and other multiplication skills will help them to do this mentally.
- Review and check findings. Ask: *Which of the heights were hardest to calculate? How were your times tables useful for this?*

EXTEND

Display digital file 22 (Who shrunk teacher?) on which the shrunken heights of all the teachers have been reorganised. Ask children to investigate which teachers will be turned into giants, and which ones may still be too small.

LOSING YER MARBLES!

You need: resource 12b (Ratio: Losing yer marbles!); snap cubes

STEPS

- Demonstrate that a ratio of 1 : 2 pink cubes to yellow cubes would mean that for 12 pink we would have 24 yellow, and so on.
- Show that ratios can come in 3s or more, such as 1 : 2 : 3 giving, for example 1 pink cube, 2 yellow and 3 green cubes. This can also give us 6 pink : 12 yellow : 18 green etc
- Look at varying amounts, eliciting the importance of the times tables in finding these. Ask: *How do your times tables facts help you to find different amounts for a certain ratio?*
- Distribute resource 12b (Ratio: Losing yer marbles!). Discuss the task and the first column of numbers. Ask: *What does this tell us,* and *how were these numbers found?*
- Display the ratio 1 : 3 : 4. Ask: *Compared to the example in the first column (1 : 4 : 5), will there be more or fewer red marbles?* (more) Also, *will we be able to put 100 marbles in this bag?* (No, because 1 + 3 + 4 = 8, and 8 is not a factor of 100; the nearest factor without going over 100 will be 96.)
- Decide whether to explain the easiest approach to finding the quantities, or to let the children investigate. (The best approach to this work is to add the 3 ratios – in this case 1 + 3 + 4 = 8 – and then find out how many 8s can go up to 100 (12 × 8 = 96). This tells us we are working in multiples of 12. So, for 1 : 3 : 4 we will have 12 : 36 : 48, and 12 + 36 + 48 = 96.)
- Allow time to complete the table, and then discuss findings. Ask: *Which were the most difficult ratios to deal with?* (The last 2 go beyond 12 × 12.)

ANSWERS:

Ratio	1:4:5	1:3:5	1:9:2	3:6:2	1:2:3	2:2:3
Number of red marbles	10	11	8	27	16	28
Number of blue marbles	40	33	72	54	32	28
Number of green marbles	50	55	16	18	48	42
Total number of marbles	100	99	96	99	96	98

EXTEND

Present lower ratios to be explored, such as 1 : 1 : 2 then 3 : 0 : 1 and 1 : 2 : 3.

A CERTAIN RATIO

You need: snap cubes or counters

STEPS

- Explain that ratio compares amounts.
- Draw white and black beads on the board in the ratio 1 : 2. (Be careful not to confuse this with proportion, which would say that 1 in 3 beads are white.)

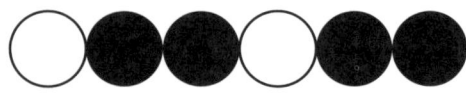

- Draw another white bead and another 2 black beads. Elicit that the ratio remains the same, 1 : 2. Ask: *If there were 24 black beads, how many white beads would there be?* (12) *What if there were 9 white beads?* (18 black).
- Provide groups of children with a good quantity of snap cubes or counters, ideally just of 2 colours, and ask each child to create a 2-colour ratio pattern – it might be 1 : 3 or 1 : 5, or something more complex such as 2 : 3 or 3 : 7. If possible, challenge the children to ensure that everyone in their group makes a different ratio.
- Explain that each child must now investigate their ratio for differing numbers within the limit of the times tables (144 max), for example a ratio of 2 : 3 might show that 30 red cubes will mean 45 yellow cubes. But 100 red cubes cannot be achieved as this would require 150 yellow cubes.
- Discuss findings. Ask: *Is a ratio with 1 as the first number easier? Why is this? Were there any numbers you couldn't calculate? If so, why not?* The 144 limit reduces options and ratios not using 1 (for example 2 : 3), relying on choosing multiples of the lower number (for example 7 would not be possible for the lower ratio in 2 : 3 because it is not a multiple of 2).

EXTEND

For their chosen ratios, ask children to try to find much larger amounts, increasing the times tables facts by 1 or more powers of 10 (for example 250 red cubes provides 375 yellow at 2 : 3).

MIND YOUR Ps AND Qs

You need: resource 2 (Times tables square)

STEPS

- Write a small selection of 'missing number' times tables facts on the board, such as 3 × __ = 6, 5 × __ = 20; __ × 4 = 16; __ × 6 = 30, and so on.
- Work with the class to insert the missing numbers, then rewrite them on the board using letters instead of blanks: 3 × p = 6, 5 × q = 20; r × 4 = 16; t × 6 = 30, then elicit the values for each letter (p = 2, q = 4; r = 4; t = 5).
- Discuss how the letter is really a missing number, then re-write 1 final time without the multiplication symbol: $3p$ = 6, $5q$ = 20; $4r$ = 16; $6t$ = 30, and elicit the value of each letter. Explain that, with algebra, the multiplication sign is not shown, and conventionally we always put the letter second ($6t$ not $t6$).
- Using times tables square (resource 2) if needed, children work in pairs to ask quick-fire algebra facts to each other, for example $4k$ = 36; $9m$ = 72; $5r$ = 55; $3b$ = 18, and so on. You may wish to limit the facts to certain tables or allow them to choose any facts up to 12 × 12.
- Demonstrate a 2-letter statements, such as yz = 55 and work through the implications of such a statement (y and z must equal 5 and 11, but either letter can be either number).
- Work through options for pq = 8; and jk = 49. Ask: *How do I know that for pq = 8, p and q can have 4 different values each, yet for jk = 49 each letter can only have 1 value lower than 12?* (Also, encourage the children to notice that j and k both have the same value. It is acceptable for different letters to have the same missing value.)
- Children can now investigate, in pairs, a selection of 2-letter times tables facts, such as ab = 36; lm = 15; rs = 72.

EXTEND

A more complex investigation can be initiated by providing algebraic sums. Still focusing only on times tables facts, present a range of sums, such as $4h + 2k$ = 16 (h = 3, k = 2; or h = 2, k = 4; or h = 1, k = 6). Children must investigate and present all possible outcomes.

abc

PAGES 34 AND 35

You need: resource 12c (Algebra: *abc*)

STEPS

- Write out '*pqr* = 6'.
Ask: *What 3 numbers multiplied together give us 6?* In discussion, elicit that this can be 1 × 2 × 3 = 6 and 1 × 1 × 6 = 6. (Note that different letters can have the same value as each other.)
- Focusing on the former calculation, spend time looking at all the options for each letter, namely 1 × 2 × 3 = 6, 2 × 1 × 3 = 6, 1 × 3 × 2 = 6, 2 × 3 × 1 = 6, 3 × 2 × 1 = 6, 3 × 1 × 2 = 6, reinforcing the commutative law. Ask: *What does this mean for algebra?* (Each letter might have more than 1 value, and if any letter changes value, so do the others.)
- Distribute resource 12c (Algebra: ***abc***) and look at the first column, demonstrating that for ***abc*** = 24, 2 × 3 × 4 = 24. Ensuring that children understand the calculation presented, ask: *What other values might each letter take?* As well as variations in order (for example 4 × 2 × 3 = 24), there are other options (for example 1 × 8 × 3, 6 × 2 × 2).
- Children should complete the table in pairs or groups to investigate each ***abc*** statement, either choosing 1 number per letter, or on separate paper tabulating the various possibilities. Ask: *Is there a quick way to identify all of the options available to you? Would it be easier or harder if 1 was not allowed as 1 of the numbers?*

EXTEND

Provide algebraic sums that focus only on times tables facts for children to investigate, such as ***ab*** + ***pq*** = 40, emphasising that all letters can only take values from 1–12. This is a very open ended activity, which can be slightly restrained by also stipulating that no 2 letters are allowed to have the same value in this activity.

KERCHING!

You need: digital file 23 (Kerching); plastic coins and imitation bank notes (optional); resource 5 (Knick-knacks) (optional)

STEPS

- Display digital file 23 (Kerching). Ask how these might relate to times tables facts.
- Either using resource 5 (Knick-knacks) as a template, or inventing your own items, display a set of items with prices lower than 12p (or £12), and use quick-fire questions to generate random tables facts (for example *model figures are 8p, how much would 9 figures cost?*).
- Explain the main focus of the activity – not to find answers, but to present explanations as to how accurate answers would be found. Demonstrate a calculation for example 6 items at £8.50 each:
    - Define the calculation: 6 × £8.50
    - Break down the calculation: 6 × £8 and 6 × 50p
    - Do both multiplications (discussing use and application of tables): £48 + 300p
    - Convert pence to pounds: 300p = £3, then add the 2 (£51)
- Present a range of single-step money calculations that sit outside, but relate to, the times tables, from easy to hard (for example 13 apples at 9p each; 20 books at £7 each), moving on to trickier prices as in the example above (for example 7 items for £2.60 each). Emphasise that the answer is not the focus of the activity, just the procedure.

EXTEND

Tie the work in to larger numbers by setting prices as multiples of pounds, with or without pence, such as £60, £490, £3000, £2.35, £12.54, and so on.

THINK!

You need: resource 13 (Across the curriculum)

STEPS

- Distribute resource 13 (Across the curriculum).
- Look at the first section and take 2 pieces of information (for example kitten: 1.2kg; puppy 6kg), and consider how simple problems might be created using 1 or both pieces of information, for example *How much would 3 puppies weigh?* Or, *How much do 5 kittens weigh?*
- Explain that you are not looking for answers. For the chosen problems say: *Explain how you would solve this problem.*
- Work with the class to write the steps for solving the problems. Ask: *How can times tables facts be used to help solve these problems?*
- Work with the class to model several questions and answers, such as:
    - *How much do 5 kittens weigh?*
    - *We know kittens weigh 1.2kg, so we can use 12-times table facts:*
    - *2 × 1.2 = 2.4, 3 × 1.2 = 3.6 … 5 × 1.2 = 6.0*
    - *So 5 kittens weigh 6kg*
- Working in pairs, explain that the children's task is to use a particular set of data, or more than 1 if preferred, to create 5 single-step problems that they must be able to do themselves. As well as the problem, they should also make a separate note of how to solve it, citing which times tables knowledge is needed.
- Ask: *How did you decide how hard your problems should be? What limited your decisions?*
- Allow children to solve each other's problems.

EXTEND

Children who have grasped the approach can be moved on to 2-step problems, for example *How much more do 20 kittens weigh than 3 puppies?*

1 SMALL STEP, 1 GIANT LEAP

You need: resource 14 (Multi-step problems)

STEPS

- Display the opening problems on resource 14 (Multi-step problems). Explain that the objective is not to answer the problems, only to explain *how* to solve them.
- Discuss the issue involved with calculating measures and that units often need converting, which can add a layer of complexity.
- Look at the first problem (involving sticks of different lengths) and model the steps to solve it: calculate the total length of small sticks, then the total length of large sticks, and then add them together.
- Look at the second problem and ask: *Why is this more complex than the first problem?* (It has an additional step at the end that requires both a change of units (that is 1 metre = 100cm) and a different operation: subtraction.
- Organising the class as desired. Children should list and explain the steps involved to solve each problem.

EXTEND

Children can progress to writing their own problems. To really fine-tune their skills, set them a definite number of steps: 3 or even 4. Typically, the more steps there are, the more complex the calculation.

WHAT'S WHAT?

You need: resource 14 (Multi-step problems)

STEPS

- Explain that this activity follows on from the previous activity, '1 small step, 1 giant leap'.
- Distribute resource 14 (Multi-step problems).
- Work through the first 2 problems with the class, discussing the steps to be taken in solving the problem before modelling how to neatly lay out the mathematics and present a correct solution.
- Children can now work through the problems individually, ensuring that for each 1 they layout the stages clearly.
- Review the work together and, for each question, highlight the times tables facts used in solving it, discussing instances where division was required as well as application of the tables facts to aid more complex calculations.

EXTEND

Children write their own problems. Ask them to look at the worksheet for reference and for ideas. Allow them time to plan and ensure that their problems are around the same difficultly level as those on the worksheet.

EXTENDING AND APPLYING THE TABLES: USING THE TABLES ACROSS THE CURRICULUM

12 × 12 TIMES TABLES SQUARE

	1	2	3	4	5	6	7	8	9	10	11	12
1	1	2	3	4	5	6	7	8	9	10	11	12
2	2	4	6	8	10	12	14	16	18	20	22	24
3	3	6	9	12	15	18	21	24	27	30	33	36
4	4	8	12	16	20	24	28	32	36	40	44	48
5	5	10	15	20	25	30	35	40	45	50	55	60
6	6	12	18	24	30	36	42	48	54	60	66	72
7	7	14	21	28	35	42	49	56	63	70	77	84
8	8	16	24	32	40	48	56	64	72	80	88	96
9	9	18	27	36	45	54	63	72	81	90	99	108
10	10	20	30	40	50	60	70	80	90	100	110	120
11	11	22	33	44	55	66	77	88	99	110	121	132
12	12	24	36	48	60	72	84	96	108	120	132	144

12 × 12 BLANK TIMES TABLES SQUARE

	1	2	3	4	5	6	7	8	9	10	11	12
1												
2												
3												
4												
5												
6												
7												
8												
9												
10												
11												
12												

100 SQUARE

1	2	3	4	5	6	7	8	9	10
11	12	13	14	15	16	17	18	19	20
21	22	23	24	25	26	27	28	29	30
31	32	33	34	35	36	37	38	39	40
41	42	43	44	45	46	47	48	49	50
51	52	53	54	55	56	57	58	59	60
61	62	63	64	65	66	67	68	69	70
71	72	73	74	75	76	77	78	79	80
81	82	83	84	85	86	87	88	89	90
91	92	93	94	95	96	97	98	99	100

NUMBER WALL

QUICK TESTS FOR SATs SUCCESS

BOOST YOUR CHILD'S CONFIDENCE WITH 10-MINUTE SATs TESTS

- Bite-size mini SATs tests which take just 10 minutes to complete
- Covers key National Test topics
- Full answers and progress chart provided to track improvement
- Available for Years 1 to 6

Find out more at www.scholastic.co.uk